Scrapbooking Basics
FOR
DUMMIES®
ULTRA-PRO EDITION

by Jeanne Wines-Reed
and Joan Wines

WILEY

Wiley Publishing, Inc.

Scrapbooking Basics For Dummies® Ultra-PRO Edition
Published by
Wiley Publishing, Inc.
111 River St.
Hoboken, NJ 07030-5774
www.wiley.com

Copyright © 2004 by Wiley Publishing, Inc., Indianapolis, Indiana

Published simultaneously in Canada

WILEY

About the Authors

Jeanne Wines-Reed is a wife, mother, artist, entrepreneur, publisher, and author. She holds an undergraduate degree in art and a graduate degree in education administration.

Jeanne enjoyed teaching art in the public schools for many years. In 1996, she left education and founded the Great American Scrapbook Company, a company that hosts the world's largest scrapbook convention. Jeanne started a second company, the International Scrapbook Trade Association (ISTA), in 1998 and published an ISTA scrapbook trade magazine. With the launching of another publication in 2002, the *Scrapbook Retailer* magazine, Jeanne has fulfilled a longtime goal of providing a venue in which scrapbook manufacturers can exchange information and expertise with scrapbook industry retailers.

Jeanne attributes her success in all of these endeavors to the support of the manufacturers in the industry. As Jeanne continues to promote scrapbooking by writing, speaking, and teaching at scrapbook consumer and trade shows, she takes her company's mission statement, *"Encouraging the Preservation of Personal and Family Histories,"* with her. She's affectionately been dubbed "The Ambassador of Good Will for Scrapbooking" because of her tireless efforts to promote scrapbooking.

Jeanne likes to point out that scrapbooking crosses every socioeconomic background in the world. "Each of us," she's fond of saying, "has a story to tell. Tell your story. People are waiting to hear it."

For more information on Jeanne Wines-Reed, please call *Scrapbook Retailer* magazine at (801) 627-3700 or visit www.greatamericanscrapbook.com.

Joan Wines, an English professor with a Ph.D. from the University of Southern California, has been working with her daughter Jeanne on publications and other facets of Jeanne's scrapbooking enterprises since 1996.

As a mother, grandmother, and member of a large extended family, Joan has an avid interest in scrapbooking personal and family histories. As a professor who teaches literature and writing, she has an equally avid interest in narrative — and thus also in the stories that scrapbooks tell.

In her professional life, besides teaching, Dr. Wines directs a Center for Teaching and Learning at California Lutheran University. She writes and presents papers on teaching and learning at national and international conferences, and is particularly interested in the integration of technologies into the higher education curriculum.

Publisher's Acknowledgments

We're proud of this book; please send us your comments through our Dummies online registration form located at www.dummies.com/register/.

Some of the people who helped bring this book to market include the following:

Acquisitions, Editorial, and Media Development

Senior Project Editor: Zoë Wykes

Editorial Manager: Rev Mengle

Cover Photo: Twede Photography

Cartoons: Rich Tennant,
www.the5thwave.com

Production

Project Coordinator: Kristie Rees

Layout and Graphics: Denny Hager, LeAndra Hosier, Stephanie D. Jumper, Michael Kruzil, Kristin McMullan, Brent Savage, Jacque Schneider, Julie Trippetti

Proofreaders: Andy Hollandbeck, Linda Quigley, Dwight Ramsey

Indexer: Johnna VanHoose

Special Help
Gabriele McCann

Publishing and Editorial for Consumer Dummies

Diane Graves Steele, Vice President and Publisher, Consumer Dummies

Joyce Pepple, Acquisitions Director, Consumer Dummies

Kristin A. Cocks, Product Development Director, Consumer Dummies

Michael Spring, Vice President and Publisher, Travel

Brice Gosnell, Associate Publisher, Travel

Kelly Regan, Editorial Director, Travel

Publishing for Technology Dummies

Andy Cummings, Vice President and Publisher, Dummies Technology/ General User

Composition Services

Gerry Fahey, Vice President of Production Services

Debbie Stailey, Director of Composition Services

Table of Contents

Introduction

*I*n this book, we categorize everything under the scrapbooking sun. But — life's not lived in categories and scrapbooking's not done in categories either. Therefore, we hope that you process well the information in *Scrapbooking Basics For Dummies,* Ultra-PRO Edition. We also hope that you allow the information to incorporate itself naturally into the whole of your scrapbooking experience.

No matter how much scrapbooking experience you have, this book is for you. You get fresh ideas and perspectives on how scrapbookers preserve their memories. If you're new to scrapbooking, you satisfy your curiosity about what goes on in the scrapbook world and identify your special interests at the same time. Try out the ideas that resonate with you and return another day to those that don't.

About This Book

Scrapbooking Basics For Dummies, Ultra-PRO Edition, takes a lot of the guesswork out of how to create an attractive scrapbook album. In this book, we walk you through the organizational process, giving you tips on how to choose your albums, paper colors for your page layouts, page materials, and tools — and we tell you about a foolproof way to design your layouts. In no time, you'll be creating beautiful pages that your family and friends will enjoy and pass on to succeeding generations.

Foolish Assumptions

We made some assumptions about you as we wrote this book:

  ✔ You know that a scrapbook includes photographs and memorabilia.

> ✔ You've probably already attempted scrapbooking, perhaps weren't satisfied with the results, and want more information on how to make an attractive, well-designed album.
>
> ✔ You're interested in finding out more about the wonderful world of scrapbooking.
>
> ✔ Family and friends are an important part of your life, and you would like to preserve your personal and family histories for future generations.

How This Book Is Organized

Scrapbooking Basics For Dummies, Ultra-PRO Edition, is divided into three parts, each of which covers a different aspect of scrapbooking. You don't have to read the book from cover to cover, although you may want to read the first chapter to get an overview of the basics of scrapbooking. After that, feel free to use the Table of Contents and the Index to read what we have to say about your particular areas of interest.

Because the book is arranged in a modular fashion, you can jump in wherever you want. But even though each section is written to stand on its own, the book also flows well from chapter to chapter, and you may prefer to read it from start to finish.

Part 1: The Amazing World of Scrapbooking

If you want to gain a better understanding of scrapbooking, you want to read this part. We tell you all about the different styles of scrapbooking, how to lay out your scrapbook pages, how to organize all the photos you have stashed in those shoe boxes, and how to organize your memorabilia. We help you discover what your purpose may be for a particular scrapbooking project and give you tips about how to create unity in your albums.

Part II: Materials Matter

If you'd like to get an overview of all of the products that go with scrapbooking, if you like matching fabrics and colors, and if you want a list of shopping guidelines that will save you time and money, this section of the book is definitely for you.

As you discover how to choose albums that are just right for you and find out how to make sure that your adhesives, papers, and other materials pass archival muster, you'll become increasingly confident about your ability to create a beautiful scrapbook album. Reading about the techniques you can try by using specific cutting tools, die-cuts, punches, stickers, stamps, pens, embellishments, and more will inspire you to pick a project and see it through to completion.

Part III: The Part of Tens

In this section, we give you a couple of handfuls of ideas on how to journal in your scrapbooks. We want to encourage you to record those funny and not-so-funny things that have been important to *you* in your life's journey. Notice the emphasis on *you*. If you remember that *your* perspective is valuable, you'll have the inside track on scrapbook journaling, since journaling is all about what *you* think and feel and love.

Check out the scrapbooking URLs in this section too. We include some of our favorite scrapbooking Web sites with a mind's eye to guessing which sites would be most interesting and helpful to you.

Icons Used in This Book

Throughout the book, you'll notice little symbols in the margin. These symbols, known as *icons,* mark important points that you'll want to note.

This bull's-eye appears next to shortcuts and tips that make your work easier.

When you see this icon, be sure that you read the paragraph. This icon warns you of common mistakes and ways to avoid them.

This icon marks any point you'll want to remember. You may even want to reread these paragraphs.

Text next to this icon is, well, technical — and sometimes difficult to follow. Feel free to skip material next to this icon if you'd like.

Where to Go from Here

Like all *For Dummies* books, this book is written as a reference book. You can dip into a chapter, come out again, and reenter later. All at your own pace and convenience. You can use the Index and Table of Contents to find the particular information you're looking for at any given time.

If you've never scrapbooked before, we recommend that you start with Part I. If you've already done some scrapbooking, you may want to read the more in-depth information in Part II. Or dive in deeper by browsing the Web sites in Part III —where you find out more (and more and more) about the great world of scrapbooking.

Part I

The Amazing World of Scrapbooking

The 5th Wave   By Rich Tennant

PAPER TECHNIQUES FOR SCRAPBOOKING

Please, Darlene, let me finish tracing your face for my scrapbook.

In this part . . .

You discover that scrapbooking involves a lot more than just pasting photos into family albums. In fact, many scrapbookers have rather "lofty" purposes and goals, describing what they do as giving something to the future by preserving the past. The added bonus is that by scrapbooking, you too can benefit because the dual acts of creating and giving are bound to bring you joy.

Chapter 1

Discovering Your Scrapbook Style

In This Chapter

▶ Deciding what kind of album to make

▶ Getting familiar with today's scrapbook styles

▶ Doing your own thing

1 n this chapter, we give you information about many different ways to approach scrapbooking. After you look at the options, you'll be in a good position to decide what kind of album(s) you want to make and how you'll integrate your own style into your work.

Figuring Out What Scrapbooking Means to You

No matter what scrapbooking ends up meaning to you, your efforts will mean something to someone else: your children, your spouse, your descendants. Everyone has a story — and not just one, but many. Which of your stories will you decide to scrapbook? How will you interpret your personal and family histories? What you've learned from those histories will have a strong impact as your insights unfold on the pages of your albums.

People make all kinds of scrapbooks. This list identifies some of the more common ways to approach scrapbooking and gives you an overview of a number of your options.

- ✔ **Documenting events and milestones:** Scrapbookers create pages and albums about every conceivable event and milestone. The industry creates themed products that work well with all of these pages and albums. Whether you're "scrapping" graduations, birthdays, confirmations, weddings, or travels, you can find stickers, stamps, and lots of other materials to go on your pages.

- ✔ **Focusing on individual biographies:** These albums focus on the life of one family member, maybe an illustrious or infamous one, maybe not.

- ✔ **Illustrating an autobiography:** The number of pages (or, more probably albums) you need to scrapbook the highlights of your life depends in part on how much memorabilia and how many photos you've collected over the years. To tell the story of your life, look carefully at the photos that mark its milestones. Try to recapture the feelings and thoughts associated with those photos by journaling — before the thoughts and feelings fade away and the memories recede. (See Chapter 8 for suggestions on a variety of journaling techniques.)

- ✔ **"Speaking out" from your scrapbook:** Your scrapbook can be a place to make your voice heard and to influence your children, your grandchildren, and many others. The albums you make can document your travels, successes, school activities, relocations, losses, and so many other things.

- ✔ **Promoting healing:** Many a scrapbook has served as therapy for those experiencing pain, suffering, and loss. The terminally ill often scrapbook their lives, and many people scrapbook the lives of lost loved ones. These examples are only a couple of the ways that scrapbooking is used to help heal. The scrapbook industry spearheads many projects that promote healing. One such project involved sending box loads of scrapbooking materials to Colorado — so that every one of the Columbine students had the opportunity to make a scrapbook. Letters from the students and their parents told how beneficial that activity had been in helping the students through their responses to tragedy.

✔ **Recording an illustrated family history:** In an album that records just the facts (dates of births, baptisms, confirmations, marriages, and deaths), you can include one identifying picture of each family member. These albums are like glorified genealogies that chart family history as far back as possible.

✔ **Setting examples:** Others can gain insight and strength from your personal scrapbooks. You can show and explain, by photos and journaling, how you've overcome challenges and obstacles. These glimpses into your life are like nuggets of gold.

Scrutinizing Some Scrapbooking "Styles"

Scrapbooking style isn't really formally definable. Styles are as individual as scrapbookers themselves, and scrappers are constantly experimenting with new looks and techniques. To give you a feel for what's going on in scrapbooking as of this writing, though, we've created some arbitrary style categories. Take a look and see which of these seems to best match your own "style."

Like other scrapbookers, you'll soon be adopting and adapting these and many other different styles — and, of course, creating a style of your very own at the same time.

Shooting with the shutter bugs

Many people who like taking photographs are drawn to scrapbooking. You can tell by glancing at their albums that the photos are what matter to them. Their pages prioritize the photo or photos, as shown in Figure 1-1, and they accessorize minimally — if at all.

Figure 1-1: A shutterbug's layout.

As you continue scrapbooking, you'll want to *(and will)* become a better photographer. Scrapbookers tend to take photography more seriously as they advance in their skills.

Analyzing the "artiste"

To look through a scrapbook artist's albums is like taking a stroll through a museum. Artistry is predominant on the pages, as shown in Figure 1-2. These scrapbookers often use tools and techniques that an artist might use, while making certain that their tools and materials are archivally safe (see Chapter 7 for more on these tools). Scrapbooking manufacturers are following this trend and have begun to create products for this style of scrapbooking.

Photo courtesy of Making Memories

Figure 1-2: The artiste's masterpiece.

Cropping with the crafty

If you like crafts, craft accouterments, and detail, you'll like the craftsperson style, shown in Figure 1-3. Craft-oriented scrapbookers like to include traditional crafting mediums and techniques such as acrylic paints, wood charms, and fabrics on their pages.

Creating classics

A "classic" anything transcends historical fads and fashions. The classic scrapbook style exudes timelessness, and the classicists in scrapbooking aim for a clean, uncluttered look, using traditional design elements. The tasteful page of a scrapbook created in a classic style has universal appeal, as shown in Figure 1-4.

Figure 1-3: A crafty scrapper's 12" x 12" layout.

Figure 1-4: A classy page.

Handling the heritage style

Heritage albums differ from illustrated family history albums in that they include more than "just the facts" and basic photos. Instead, your memorabilia, photos, and themes suggest "heritage" both in color and design. Crinkled papers, pieces of lace, and other such materials create historical context for your contents. The journaling is also a great way to share snippets about your ancestors' lives, as shown in Figure 1-5.

Figure 1-5: Discovering more about the family ancestors.

Sure, you can do Shabby Chic

Shabby Chic albums feel comfortable, cozy, and homey. The look is vintage and worn. Lots of peeling furniture, old china, tendrils, flowers, and pastels. Torn, stitched, and inked papers are commonly found in these albums. Shabby Chic pages are eclectic and fun, as shown in Figure 1-6.

Photo courtesy of Making Memories

Figure 1-6: Shabby but chic.

Making it modern

Albums in the modern style tend to have geometric shapes, angular lines, and bold colors. Designs look clean and are usually executed with a few well-placed lines or shapes, as shown in Figure 1-7.

Putting up with pop

The pop style is what you might expect — edgy, fun, contemporary. Lots of little metal doodads (like eyelets and brads) punched through the papers, as shown in Figure 1-8. Pop scrapbookers use the newest and most innovative products — from metal frames and charms, ribbons and fibers to beads and buttons. (See Chapter 7 to find out more about accessorizing your scrapbook albums with trendy embellishments.)

Figure 1-7: The clean-lined, minimalist, modern look.

Photo courtesy of Making Memories

Figure 1-8: The trendy, light-metal culture.

Knowing Your Purpose

Some people scrapbook because they love the craft. Others are focused on preservation and are concerned about the archival aspects of scrapbooking — thinking always about how long their albums will last. These folks take seriously their purpose of leaving a legacy for future generations, so quality materials (like pigment-based journaling pens) are very important to them (for more on archival materials, see Part II). Other scrapbookers care more about highlighting their current family events — for the enjoyment of those people who are living *now*.

Aside from the overall purpose(s) you may have for scrapbooking, you'll find that you also have a specific purpose for every scrapbook you make. For example, you may simply want to save a memory (of a favorite grandparent, or of that great vacation you thought you'd never get to take, but finally did).

Understanding your general and specific purposes for scrapbooking will help you make better decisions about the direction of your work.

Going About the "Shoot and Tell"

Sure, photos are just quick little slices of your life experiences, but the *way* you *shoot* (take pictures) and *tell* (journal) lays the foundation for the unique characteristics of your scrapbooking style.

Shooting the scene

Which do you like better — taking pictures of flowers or of people? Would you rather photograph a single person or a group of people? Do you like to take close-ups or distance shots? Portrait or landscape angles? Color or black and white? Do you shoot, shoot, shoot and pick out the best of the bunch later, or are you conservative with your film? Answering these questions will tell you some things about the characteristics of your personal photo-taking perspectives.

Not that you'll limit yourself to any one particular way of taking photographs. In December, you may shoot 20 rolls of film of family groups partying during the holidays. At another time, you may take a set of dynamite close-up photos of your new baby.

Haul your camera with you all the time. Take it everywhere you go. Photograph the major events in your personal life and the lives of your family and friends: birthdays, weddings, travels, relocations — and all other events you value.

Telling the tale

A picture may be worth a thousand words, but still, your photos can only say so much. You *need* to tell the stories that go with your photographs. Tuck a journal into your camera case or bag, so that you can jot down details about the photos you take. The feelings and moods that prompt you to take a photo quickly pass so you need to capture them before they're gone forever. Later, you can copy your words onto the scrapbook page to enhance the story that your photos tell.

Journaling (writing on your scrapbook pages) is an important sector in the scrapbooking world. People looking at your scrapbooks want to know who's who and what's what, and industry manufacturers have created hundreds of products and techniques to help scrapbookers answer those questions on their pages. Hundreds of books on journaling and many Web sites have also been created for this purpose.

Locating Your M and Ps

Somewhere, at the backs of drawers and shelves, or tucked away in the corners and crevices of a garage, attic, or closet, you have hidden treasure, treasure we call your M and Ps — your personal and family memorabilia and photographs. When you begin scrapbooking, just *finding* your M and Ps may require a major act of willpower.

Think of searching for your M and Ps as a grand treasure hunt — one that will eventually enrich your life more than any buried treasure ever would. Your memorabilia can include anything you've saved that's small enough to put in a scrapbook: matchbooks, airline tickets, keys, house deeds, and so on. Collecting it all can certainly spice up your life. You'll come upon memorabilia items stuck in the most unlikely places and smile or shed a tear as you put the item in a "holding" place along with your other memorabilia.

After you've gone photo hunting and put all the photographs you can find in the same place, it's time to go begging. Ask your family members and friends for photos you may want but don't have, and then make copies of them.

If you're missing documents like birth, marriage, and death certificates, you can usually get copies from the counties where the events took place.

Hopefully, you'll be able to gather your memorabilia and photographs together in one place (the bigger the place, the better). Organizing your M and Ps chronologically is the next step. You can, for example, put all the M and Ps for 1970 in photo box holders or in hanging file folders. Label the boxes or files and create a list that includes the year and the major events that took place that year. You can fine-tune your organization from there when you're ready to make your albums (see Chapter 3 for more on organizing and designing your layouts).

Choosing Your Favorite Materials and Techniques

The options available in scrapbooking materials can seem overwhelming, but we give you shopping guides to help you make those choices (see Part II). Browse your local scrapbook store(s). Check out what's online. Go to a few scrapbook conventions and wander the show floor, keeping an eye out for new products and demonstrations of new techniques. You'll know what you like when you see it.

Choosing the scrapbook materials and techniques that work best for you is a matter of trial, error, and education. No matter how much information you discover about materials (and you discover a lot in Part II), you still have to try out different materials and techniques. You will also have to make a few mistakes before you know what works best for you.

Chapter 2

Before You Begin . . .

*Y*ou're going to love scrapbooking. So much so that you'll be glad you invested time and energy into finding out all you can — *before* you begin your first album. In this chapter, we give you some advice about those planning landmarks: creating a work space, collecting items for your pages, and organizing all of your materials so that your albums will have the "finished" look you want.

Settling In: Your Own Little Scrapbook World

In order to complete quality scrapbooking work, you need an orderly, inviting place to scrapbook in.

Organizing your materials and creating stories for your scrapbook(s) will be easier and more fun if you first organize a work space where you can do your scrapbooking. Give yourself permission to set up your own "studio" — a place where you can think, dream, and create.

To help you decide where that place will be, however, we give you a checklist of must-haves for your scrapbooking studio:

- ✔ **Good lighting:** Instantly professionalizes your space.
- ✔ **A comfortable chair:** Preferably an ergonomic chair in your favorite color.
- ✔ **A bulletin board (or two):** For tacking up lists, reminders, and layout ideas you get from magazines, fellow scrapbookers, Web sites, and other sources.
- ✔ **A flat, easy-to-clean working surface:** With plenty of room for a cutting mat and spreading out your stuff.
- ✔ **A good-sized filing cabinet:** Needs to accommodate 12" x 12" hanging file folders.
- ✔ **Label tags:** For the file folders.
- ✔ **A rod:** For hanging hangable supplies.

Staking your claim and creating a space

Clear a space just for you and set up shop. Take a room if you can get it, or a corner of a room, or a closet. Even a table will do. *Anywhere* that you can call your own and feel assured that your supplies won't be disturbed.

Get as much room as possible. You'll need it. You want to be able to take your supplies out, set them up, and leave them there. Putting stuff away and taking it out whenever you work takes far too much precious time.

Purchasing a pre-made "studio"

You can build your own scrapbooking-organizing system or you can buy one pre-made. Scrapbook-industry manufacturers offer options to meet any scrapper's organizational needs. Whether you have a lot of space or little to none, you'll find your organization answer somewhere within the wide range of storage and organizing choices (from fully furnished rooms to organizational backpacks).

Many companies sell pre-made home organizational systems for scrapbookers. Here's a list of just a few of the systems you may want to consider.

 ✔ The "KeepsSake Creation Station," shown in Figure 2-1, looks like a piece of furniture. It stores an entire scrap-book room behind the doors of a beautiful armoire. Scrapbook supplies are at your fingertips on a lighted desktop you can roll away — so that you don't have to disturb your pages-in-progress when you get up from your work.

 ✔ Cropper Hopper's "Home Center," shown in Figure 2-2, is a component system, each piece of which is a vertical storage module. One of the cubes for paper holds 1,200 sheets of paper, and the vertical-sticker envelopes organize stickers by theme.

Photo courtesy of For Keeps Sake

Figure 2-1: "KeepsSake Creation Station" — an in-house scrapbook studio.

Photo courtesy of Advantus Corp.

Figure 2-2: Cropper Hopper's home storage component system.

✔ "Store-in-Style" by Crop-in-Style, shown in Figure 2-3, is another modular home-storage solution. Made from laminated, medium-density fiberboard, these modules come in classic white and vintage honey. Three 16" x 16" cubes (the accessorizer, the filer, and the organizer) can be customized based on the demands of each individual hobbyist. Inserts fit into the cubes and can serve as organizational dividers.

Think inside the box . . .

Crop-in-Style's motto — "thinking inside the box" — aptly describes what your scrapbook working space is all about. You *can* think inside an organizing "box," reflect on your personal and family histories, consider their meaning, and creatively transmit your perspective to your pages. Scrapbooking offers you the rare opportunity to share your unique vision with family and friends. Your stories will touch their hearts and the hearts of others you'll never even meet.

Photo courtesy of Creativity, Inc.

Figure 2-3: "Store-in-Style" by Crop-in-Style.

Packing portable storage systems and organizers

If you're really tight on space, a portable storage system and organizer may be for you. Many of these organizers sit on a solid base with wheels and fold open, as shown in Figure 2-4. Scrapbookers can wheel their work and supplies anywhere in the house or on the road, do some sorting, cropping, or adhering, and then tuck the organizer away in a corner of a closet until the next time.

You can also purchase scrapbooking backpacks, shoulder bags, rolling bags, and other kinds of small-sized organizers. Scrapbookers pack these with their supplies and pages-in-progress and take them to conventions, scrapbook-store classes, *crops* (scrapbooking "bees"), or on personal trips. Serious scrappers have a scrapbooking bag "loaded" so that they can take their work with them at a moment's notice.

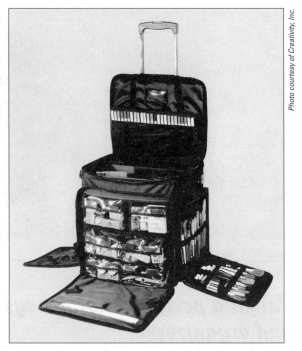

Photo courtesy of Creativity, Inc.

Figure 2-4: Wheeling around your scrapbook system.

Organizing Your Materials

Organization is the key to making pages happen — fast! In scrapbooking, you have a lot of materials to organize: memorabilia, photos, papers, stickers, die-cuts, embellishments, punches, templates, idea books, adhesives, computer software, albums, stamps, inks, tools, and more (see Part II for lots of information on materials).

As you prepare to make a specific album, the first order of the day is to organize the memorabilia and photos (M and Ps) that will go into your album.

✔ **Memorabilia:** Organizing your memorabilia in hanging folders, labeling the folders chronologically, and listing the important events for that year will save you time in the long run. Keep a list that tells you which folder each memorabilia item is in and store the list in the first file folder of your memorabilia filing system. This way you can find memorabilia quickly and access it however you want — either chronologically or by event.

✔ **Old Photos:** Collect old family photo albums from anywhere you can find them and take out all of the photographs. Do this as soon as you possibly can. Many of the old albums have already damaged their contents and are doing more damage each passing day (see Chapter 4 for information about archival standards for albums).

✔ **New Photos:** Keep on top of your more recent photos by developing the film right away. Write the date and list the contents on the envelope as soon as you pick up your developed film. Take the negatives out, place them in negative sleeves, and integrate them into your tracking sheet.

You may want to number your negative holders with the same number you've used to number your photo envelopes. You can also use these numbers to help create a tracking sheet — either on the computer or by hand.

✔ **Negatives:** Negatives last a lot longer than prints, so it's very important to organize your negatives and store them in a safe place. You can keep negatives in hanging negative holders that fit into a file cabinet or in negative sleeve preservers, a.k.a. holders.

Some scrapbookers store negatives of the photos that are in a particular album in the album itself. Invariably, someone looking through a finished album will "have to have" a print of a photo or two. Keeping the negatives right at hand makes it easier to get extra prints quickly.

✔ **CD digital photos:** If you're shooting digital, Ultra-PRO has a great system for storing your photo CDs. Their storage booklet holds the photo CD you get from the photo shop as well as your photo proofs (thumbnails of your images).

After you stake out a work space and organize your materials, you're ready to get started on the more detailed organization needed for a specific project. Here you go!!

✓ Decide what kind of an album you want to make.

✓ Put the M and Ps for that album into page protectors — four to ten M and Ps in each page protector.

✓ Approximate the number of pages you need to make the album — say that you have 100 vacation photos and you're going to do a whole album about that vacation. Will you want one or two photos on each page? Do you plan to collage some pages with four or more photos? (Chapter 4 tells you what you need to know about choosing albums.)

✓ Estimate the average number of photos per page.

✓ Estimate the number of pages you'll have in your album.

Achieving Unity in Your Albums

Unity is as critical in scrapbooking as it is in any creative work. You want your scrapbook album to look cohesive and to convey a sense of order. Unity is achieved when each part of your scrapbook page appears to be essential to the whole.

These suggestions will help you create a unified album:

✓ **Decide on a theme:** Choose the event or experience that you want to scrapbook — your summer vacation, for example. After you put your M and Ps for the album into page protectors, select an album that will go with the vacation theme.

✓ **Choose a color scheme:** You may get ideas for your color palette from your album cover, from one of your photographs, or from some other source. Keeping all the layouts in your album within the perimeters of one color palette will help give your album a unified look.

✔ **Use materials consistently:** Journal with ink colors, sticker styles, papers, and other materials that go well with the colors in your palette. Taking care with these choices pays off big time in unifying your pages.

✔ **Write the story in your own hand:** Journaling in your own handwriting is a very effective unity device for scrapbook albums.

✔ **Pick a point of view:** Choosing one point of view for the journaling in your album and staying with it throughout also helps you achieve unity. Many scrapbookers use the first person "I" point of view, but others prefer the third person "you" point of view often seen in Christmas letters.

✔ **Select the same photographic "look":** As a general rule, black-and-white photos alongside colored photographs don't contribute a unified feel to the album. Of course, a modern or pop scrapbook stylist might experiment with breaking a rule and doing so successfully. (It wouldn't be the first time in the history of scrapbooking!)

Chapter 3

Designing Your Layout

• •

• •

*B*y the time you start working on layout design for a scrapbook, you need to have (all in one place) the album, your memorabilia and photographs loosely organized in page protectors, and your papers, stickers, pens, and accessories. These materials (and knowing your purpose for making the album) help to narrow your design and style choices (refer to Chapter 1 for a quick overview of some of the most popular scrapbook styles).

Almost anything goes in scrapbook design. Any approach, any design, any style. But hey! We have a surefire, simple method for designing page layouts — and you too can develop the method in no time at all.

After laying out the materials you've chosen for your album on a clean working space — as big a space as you can get (refer to Chapter 2 for ideas on how to create a scrapbook work space), you're ready to include some traditional design elements. Using the elements of color and value, line and shape, texture and space adds unity, harmony, balance, rhythm, and beauty to your scrapbook pages.

Enriching Your Work with Color and Value

The qualities of color affect our emotions directly and immediately. These qualities also exude vitality and bring the multicolored world we live in onto our scrapbook pages.

In the following sections, we review how colors are categorized and how they relate to each other. We promise you that this information is bound to make your scrapbooking days much easier.

Reviewing the color wheel

Scrapbookers often use a lot of color in their page designs to perk up the spirit and to create excitement. Reviewing the color wheel (see Figure 3-1) reminds you of how many color choices you have and stimulates ideas about how to use color in your designs.

- ✔ **Primary colors (red, yellow, and blue):** Bold, bright, and brimming with vitality, these colors can animate and enliven your pages with their energy. Primary colors are often used on pages that feature young children, for example.

- ✔ **Secondary colors (orange, green, and violet):** Secondary colors are often used on "special-occasion" pages. Scrapbookers are big on Halloween, for example, and many manufacturers feature orange (along with black, of course) in their materials. Violet is a spring and Easter color, and you'll see lots of violet on Easter pages in scrapbook albums.

- ✔ **Complementary colors:** Complementary colors are directly opposite each other on the color wheel. Red is across from green, for example. Putting complementary colors next to each other makes each of the colors appear more intense and "vibrant." As you might expect, these particular complementary colors (red and green) are often used on Christmas holiday pages.

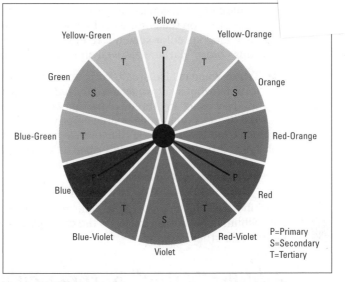

Figure 3-1: A color wheel.

> ✔ **Cool and warm colors:** You can use the cool color/
> warm color distinction in your layouts. Splitting the color
> wheel in half, from the yellow through the violet, puts
> half the colors on the warm side (red/orange side) and
> half on the cool side (blue/green group). If you're scrap-
> booking an Alaskan vacation, for example, you probably
> want to use cool colors to depict the environment.

Choosing a three-color approach

We recommend using three colors that work well together and
sticking with that color scheme throughout the album. If you
use more than three colors, your page can appear chaotic,
whereas staying within your three-color palette will make
your page appear unified and inviting.

You can choose colors just because you like the way they look
together, or you can choose your three colors based on either
of these two color schemes: an *analogous* color scheme (the
three colors are next to each other on the color wheel) or a
triad color scheme in which the three colors are *equidistant*
(an equal distance apart on the color wheel).

- ✔ **Analogous:** You can use any three colors that are next to each other on the color wheel if you want to implement an analogous color scheme (refer to Figure 3-1). Analogous colors "harmonize" well and create a definite mood.

- ✔ **Triad:** You can also create your three-color scheme by forming what's known as a *color triad.* You form a color triad by using any three colors that are separated by 120 degrees on the 360-degree color wheel. The colors in a triad color scheme (like orange, violet, and green) are colors that might be described as startling, but they're often used artistically to add impact and drama to scrapbook pages.

Your photographs help you determine an album color, and your album color in turn suggests the color palette for your papers and other materials.

Adding "value" to three-color and other basic color schemes

By including different shades of your chosen three colors, you add what artists refer to as "value." Putting a couple of other colors from the same *hue* (shade or tint of a given color) around your three main colors creates dimension and depth on your page. (You can also add black and white to darken and lighten the color value.)

Include the hues on both sides of each of the three colors in your palette. You'll find the different shades of a given color radiating from the color toward the center of the color wheel. (Refer to the color wheel in Figure 3-1 to review the hues).

You don't *have* to go the three-color route. You can try monochromatic or complementary color schemes as well.

- ✔ **Monochromatic:** You can use a *monochromatic* (a one-color) scheme and add value with multiple shades of that color.

- ✔ **Complementary:** You can use any two *complementary* colors (colors that are opposite each other on the color wheel) and add hues as you like.

If you'd rather not spend too much time figuring out a color scheme for your album, you can find ready-to-go color combination packets and easy how-to books on color schemes at your local scrapbook store.

Using Lines and Shapes

Line and shape, two of the most fundamental elements of design, can be used on your scrapbook page to lead the eye where you want it to go. These two elements are the main components of *composition* (the placement of lines and shapes and their relationship to each other on a page).

Lines

You can create lines on your page in various lengths and widths to indicate direction, to frame an area or areas, and so on. Lines also create a frame of reference within your page layout. You can either draw the lines for your frame or border, or you can *imply* the lines. To imply or suggest the lines, place items (like yarn or stickers) every so often along the border "line." Whether you use a solid border or simply imply a border, leave an inch or so of space between the border and the outside edges of the page.

Planning your composition — and a scrapbook version of the golden mean

Lines are crucial when composing an art piece by using a design concept known as the *golden mean* — a concept that, when applied, helps ensure good composition and balance. *Note:* We've adjusted the golden mean concept a little, so that we can apply it specifically to scrapbook page design.

To design a page by using the "scrapbook golden mean concept," begin by imagining that four lines (two vertical and two horizontal) divide your page into a tick-tack-toe grid (see Figure 3-2). The lines create nine spaces (or cells or boxes) on your page.

Photo courtesy of Brenda Walton for K & Company

Figure 3-2: An imaginary "tick-tack-toe" grid on your page.

The eye is naturally drawn to the four places where your imaginary grid lines intersect. These intersections become your composition's *focal points,* the points over which you want to position your strongest, most important items.

You can, for example, center a dominant photo right over one of these intersections, and a second photo, memorabilia item, or embellishment on another.

By placing one of your three main colors over a golden mean intersection, you provide interest and unity to your design. By framing a photo with a mat in your color palette, you add impact and polish to your pages.

If you use a journaling tag or card on your page, put it over one of the upper-level intersections (for more on using tags and cards for journaling, see Chapter 8). A journaling note is *lighter* (less visually dense) than a photograph, and you want only the *heavier* (more visually absorbing and demanding) items over the two lower intersection points.

Putting heavier items toward the lower sections of your composition mimics and reinforces our perception of the gravitational world we live in — where material objects are "grounded."

Designing is more efficient (and the layout designs are bigger) if you use a two-page spread. Treat a two-page spread as one big rectangular layout (see Figure 3-3).

When you design a two-page spread (which we strongly recommend you do whenever possible), imagine the golden mean grid lying across both pages. Then treat the two pages as one design.

Figure 3-3: Golden mean grid on a two-page spread.

Creating balance

Balance is achieved by equalizing the weights of the items you place on a page. If you put a "heavy" shape in one place, you can create balance by grouping a few small things together somewhere else to distribute weight equally throughout your composition.

✓ Grouping items gives them weight.

✓ *Juxtaposing* (putting side by side or close together) a very light shape with a heavy shape creates a sense of imbalance.

✓ Making the bottom border of your page a bit thicker than the other three sides of the border is a neat little balancing trick. This weights the bottom of the page, creates a grounded feeling, and keeps the eye inside the page borders.

✓ Don't divide your page into four equal parts, put an important object right in the middle, or send your lines (whether straight, horizontal, vertical, diagonal, or curved) toward any of the four corners. Doing so alienates rather than engages your viewers because it runs the eye right to the edge of the page and then outside of it.

Shapes

Using a variety of geometric and or organic shapes on your page can add interest to your layout. Place shapes where the four golden mean lines intersect — centering the shapes right over the intersections points.

The photographs you choose may themselves suggest shapes you want to use on your scrapbook page. Taking your cue from there, you want to use similar types of shapes (rectangles, circles, squares) for the layout (important when you choose your stickers, die-cuts, and other items). By using the same kinds of shapes, you add a sense of unity and balance to your pages.

Shapes can be *conveyed* (communicated) through patches of color or texture, as well as through accessories (for more on accessories, see Chapter 7).

When you lay a shape on your paper, you also create a negative space (the space that surrounds your shape). You can make the negative space an obvious part of your design — by shadowing it with a light hue from your color palette, for example. But don't go overboard. You want to let the negative space serve its function as a place for the eyes to pause and rest as they move around the page.

Creating Mood with Textures and Accessories

The people and events in your pictures will help you determine the mood you want your pages to convey. If you can pinpoint the mood, you can find the materials to express it. Your color scheme will itself contribute to the mood, but if you want to intensify the mood, one of the best ways to do so is to use textures.

Scrapbook manufacturers make many textured papers (such as various kinds of grass papers) and papers that have the semblance of texture; that is, the patterns in the papers look like textures. (See Chapter 6 for techniques on how to create textures with paper.)

You can also add different items to your papers to create textures that help establish certain moods. Examples include fibers, fabrics, ribbons, sand, wood, metals, and threads (such as embroidery threads). The accessories you use will reflect the feelings you want to evoke from those who will be looking at your album (see Chapter 7 for a rundown of some of the most popular scrapbook accessories).

Keep textures and textured patterns simple. If a textured pattern is too busy or intense, the pattern can become intrusive and distracting.

Making Magic with Spatial Illusions

The scrapbook page is a two-dimensional surface of height (vertical space) and width (horizontal space). You can use these spaces to create depth and perspective — the illusions of dimension — to your pages.

If your album pages are too busy, too jammed with stuff, people are likely to turn the pages quickly. Using space in a design to engage the eye is one of the oldest of the artist's magic tricks.

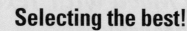

Selecting the best!

In planning the layout for a particular album, don't expect to use all the photographs you've selected for the album. Pick out the photos that have the most significance for you and then count them. By doing so, you can determine the approximate number of pages you'll be making for your album (refer to Chapter 1 for information on discovering your style, your purpose, and your organizational approach).

Here are some handy space tricks:

- ✔ Give the illusion of distance and of advancing and receding movement by manipulating the placement of items on a page and the spaces around them. (See Chapter 7 for more on composition.)

- ✔ Highlight and emphasize items by putting plenty of space around them. Give your main points of interest enough breathing room. The more important an element is to your layout, the more important it is to leave space around that element.

- ✔ Establishing enough space (about an inch) between the edges of the page and the border encourages viewers to come *into* the page — and to stay there longer. The importance of space in your design becomes evident as soon as you lay down your border lines.

Part II
Materials Matter

The 5th Wave By Rich Tennant

@RICHTENNANT

"That's my area for scrapbooking. It used
to be in the bedroom, but Martin got
tired of having the light on until
2 o'clock in the morning."

In this part . . .

We brief you on what to look for when you shop for materials for your own scrapbook. Materials *do* matter. A lot! And what matters to most of today's scrapbookers is archival quality. Which materials, over time, do the least amount of damage to memorabilia and photos? That's the question. And you're about to find out the answer.

Chapter 4

Albums, Adhesives, and Page Protectors

Scrapbookers buy, collect, and create albums of all sizes and shapes to preserve their photographs and memorabilia. Scrapbooking enthusiasts find albums everywhere — at scrapbook conventions, in scrapbook and photography stores, online at scrapbooking Web sites, and in gift shops. (See Chapter 9 for details about hot shopping spots.)

In this chapter, we give you tips on choosing the albums that are right for you, and we clue you in on buying and using adhesives and page protectors. We also give you shopping lists to guide you through the aisles.

Choosing Your Album

Scrapbook albums are as diverse as their contents — and almost as numerous. To help keep all the information about albums straight, think first about categorizing albums as either *expandable* or *bound*.

Considering expandable albums

Expandable bindings let you take pages out, put pages in, and move pages around in your album. You can add new pages and easily re-sequence your original layouts. And, as you may have guessed, expandable binders can be broken down into further categories:

✔ **Post-bound albums:** A post-bound album has a set of screws that can be tightened into and loosened from the binding. Extension posts can be fastened to the existing post screws to expand the album. These albums, as shown in Figure 4-1, are our personal favorites. They come in a generous assortment of sizes (currently 5" x 7" to 12" x 15") and a wide range of prices (anywhere from $13 to $38). You generally can interchange the standardized pages of post-bound albums made by different companies.

These albums lie somewhat flat when open — there's no metal bar sticking up between the pages to distract from the artistry of the layout. *And*, most manufacturers include several pages plus page protectors when you purchase the album.

Photo courtesy of Scrapbook Retailer magazine

Figure 4-1: A post-bound album.

✔ **Strap-hinge albums:** A simple staple strap in the binding holds the pages of the strap-hinge album in place. Sold in a variety of sizes, these sturdy albums are expensive but extremely durable. They almost always include pages and page protectors, and, like the post-bound albums, lie flat when open — so that the eye can move from one page to the next without a visual interruption.

You can't use a post-bound page in a strap-hinge album because the bindings are different. The post-bound album uses holes in the binding, whereas the strap-hinge uses a staple strap to hold the pages in place (See Figure 4-2).

✔ **Three-ring binders:** These binders aren't technically expandable, but you *can* expand your pages within the limits of the permanent rings. Available in several sizes, such as 8½" x 11" and 12" x 12", three-ring binders are inexpensive, easy to use, and great for getting things organized.

Figure 4-2: A strap-hinge album.

Looking into bound albums

Bound albums come in practically any size, color, and price range and are held together by a wide range of materials, such as metal, glue, ribbon, twine, and raffia. In the following list, we talk about the two opposite ends of the bound album spectrum: the reasonably inexpensive, ready-to-go, spiral-bound albums and the highly priced, leather-bound albums that are sometimes used to preserve especially valuable photos and memorabilia.

- ✔ **Spiral-bound albums** have permanent metal or plastic bindings, so you can't move their pages around. But you *can* tear pages out. These albums are both convenient and quick, and can make a terrific presentation. They're often targeted for a special occasion ("here's to memories of our day on the island") or to a specific person or persons.

- ✔ **Leather albums** are often Italian imports — bound, elegant, and expensive. Usually used for genealogies, personal histories, and special events, these albums are sold by wedding photographers, high-end gift shops, and photography stores. The typical high-end leather album costs around $700, comes with a piece of paper between each of the pages, and includes a protective briefcase.

Although preservation experts don't all agree, some have speculated that leather may have a detrimental effect on photographs over the long term.

Because the pages of a bound album are bound like the pages of a book, they don't offer the flexibility of the expandable albums described earlier.

Setting your sights on specialty albums

Albums also come in a third category called specialty albums (because of their uniqueness). Some specialty albums are expandable, whereas others are bound; some are large, while others are tiny. Specialty albums can be quite inexpensive or very pricey. Regardless, specialty albums all have the common characteristic of being, well, special.

Specialty albums are as unique and diverse as the people who make them. Many of these albums enable you to include a lot of photos in one small package; plus, they make wonderful gifts.

You can buy pre-designed specialty albums (usually bound), or you can make your own specialty albums from kits or from scratch.

✔ **Pre-designed bound albums:** Variety isn't a strong suit of pre-designed bound albums, but price is. Prices range from $9.99 to $21.99 an album. Some pre-designed albums are set up so that all you have to do is slip your pictures into the pockets and write on the lines provided for your journaling.

These albums are bound, as shown in Figure 4-3, and the pages don't come out — which is an advantage when you don't want children and other family members to "borrow" pages they might forget to return.

Figure 4-3: A pre-designed bound specialty album (closed and open).

✔ **Handmade albums:** If you want to make an album yourself, you can buy an inexpensive pre-prepared kit or template, or you can do your own binding and even make your own paper. The Paper Source store is a good place to start if you plan to create a handmade album.

- **Simple album kits:** Making your own album is relatively simple with these kits. Several companies sell them, so you'll find plenty of variety.

- **Templates:** You can use templates to create tiny albums. These templates come in a wide range of styles. They're cute, numerous, and very affordable. You can find them at most scrapbook retail stores.

- **Rollabind:** This company sells a great little machine you can use to make your own expandable album — and you choose the paper, the cover, and the size. (See Figure 4-4.)

- **Wooden album covers:** Wooden covers are inexpensive and are usually post-bound. But being made of wood complicates things. On one hand, a wooden album offers you an opportunity to be innovative. You can decorate its cover by using pens, paint, wood burnings, and other embellishments. But wood contains *lignin,* a substance that's highly detrimental to your scrapbook pages. For this reason, many scrapbookers will use various sized wooden albums for copies of photos and use safer album types for their original photos.

- **Book-bound albums:** These albums require extensive handiwork. The cost is high, but so is the sense of satisfaction you get when you create one of these priceless works of art. Many high-end art stores offer bookbinding classes for those who want to make albums from scratch.

Stockpiling albums "on sale"

Albums that you can buy "cheap" are great for storing works in progress or as "schlepping albums" — just for carrying your pages to the various places where you'll be *cropping* (trimming) your photos and memorabilia to fit your overall page design.

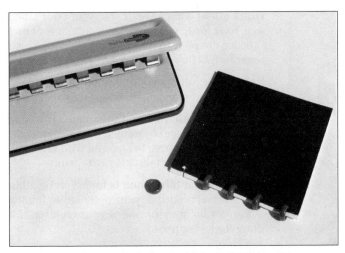

Figure 4-4: An album made by hand with the Rollabind machine.

Albums: A Shopper's Checklist

Album options today are expanding at an accelerated rate. Scrapbooking manufacturers, amazingly sensitive to the demands of creative scrapbookers, produce a wide variety of album types and styles for markets around the world. You may find the options mind-boggling when you first go to buy an album, so keep the following checklist close at hand:

✔ **Look beyond buzzwords.** Phrases like "safe for memories" don't guarantee archival quality. Instead, search for words such as *lignin free, acid-free,* and *archival* in the promotional materials that market an album. For more about these terms, see Chapter 6.

✔ **Smell the albums.** Huh? Yes, do it. Sniff the album and try to detect the smell of petroleum. An album made with a petroleum-based product emits gases that can destroy its contents. The vinyl three-ring binders that children use for schoolwork are perfect examples. Never buy a vinyl album for scrapbooking. Very deadly for your precious memories.

✔ **Think about a slipcase.** If you want your album to wear well, look for a more expensive album that includes a slipcase cover. *Note:* You seldom find slipcases sold separately. They usually come with the album, as a set.

A slipcase protects your album from light, heat, and moisture that can cause serious damage.

✔ **Look for overall quality.** Craftsmanship and materials in the stitching and binding tell a lot about the quality of an album. If an album is covered with material or canvas, make sure that the fabric is high quality.

✔ **Consider what the album is for?** Will the album be a gift, an historical record of your personal or family history, or a special album for one of your children? Match your album to its purpose.

✔ **What about size?** How much material will you want to put into your album? And what are the sizes of your memorabilia and photos? The most popular album size is 12" x 12". But sizes range from mini albums that fit on a necklace to a 16" x 16" album. (Larger albums are available, but not commonly used.)

If you use the same size scrapbooks for family and personal histories, you can exchange pages whenever you want.

✔ **Will the album lie flat?** The size of your album should accommodate the photos and memorabilia you plan to put in it so that your finished scrapbook will lie flat when open.

"Scrap" books of old ...

The twenty-first-century scrapbook album traces its lineage to two important ancestors: the photo album and the "scrap" book. In earlier centuries, photographs were kept in photo albums — period! "Scrap" books, however, were used for displaying colorful memorabilia — tidbits and "scraps" of everything imaginable. Today's scrapbook retains characteristics of both ancestors, yet still has a personality all its own. Today's scrapbook contains memorabilia *and* photographs (in abundance), but also includes personal stories, historical facts, and highly original artwork.

✔ **Choose a design and color.** More than100 manufacturers make scrapbook albums, and every one of them offers a wide range of colors and designs. Look around for the colors you like because you'll most likely be able to find them. Trust your own taste and keep an eye out for design ideas.

After you've chosen (or made) your album, you'll soon want to begin filling it with photographs. Before you start pasting, however, you need to know something about adhesives.

Adhesives: Great Stuff for the Sticky-Fingered

Knowing which adhesives to use and when to use them can make the difference between a scrapbook that lasts and one that doesn't.

In this section, we give you a lot of information on photo adhesive options — mostly because first-time scrapbookers are generally more interested in *adhering* (holding fast) photos than in adhering other scrapbook materials. But one thing often leads to another in scrapbooking, so we also talk about using adhesives for sticking papers, memorabilia (like your first corsage or ticket stubs), and other embellishments to your pages.

Sticking with the best . . .

Adhesives can be thought of as acrylic-based, rubber-based, or natural (starches and wheat pastes, for example). Professional archivists generally avoid acrylic- and rubber-based mixtures and instead opt for natural adhesives — which are *reversible* (dissolvable). But since scrapbooks "live" in everyday environments, not in museums, and the natural adhesives attract mold and other harmful organisms, natural adhesives are not the best choice for scrapbooking. Scrapbookers also avoid the rubber-based adhesives because the components in these products can separate over time. Most of the adhesives manufactured in the scrap-book industry (and there are many), are acrylic-based.

We also walk you through when and when not to use specific adhesives *and* how to "unstick" your work if you change your mind or make a mistake.

Choosing your adhesives

Obviously, adhesives play a major role in scrapbooking since everything has to be attached to the scrapbook page. But no one type or size of adhesive "fits all." Different items require different adhesives — *and* adhesives come in many forms and dispenser types.

To help you decide which adhesives to buy, we categorize them as dry or wet and removable, repositionable, or permanent.

Opting to buy dry or wet adhesives?

Dry adhesives are solids and vary widely in form and type. *Wet* adhesives are liquids and are sold in tubes or glue pens.

Dry adhesives

Because dry adhesives are easy to use and come in all sorts of scrapbooking enhancements, we prefer using dry adhesives whenever possible. Here's a list of dry-adhesive items you can buy for your albums:

- **Photo mounting corners.** These little triangular-shaped corners have adhesive on one side and paper (with lots of color options — or clear) on the other. You slip each corner of your photo into the four corner-holders so that adhesive never touches your photos.

- **Photo mounting squares.** These double-sided adhesive squares come in different sizes and a variety of dispensing types. The dry adhesive used on these squares is safe for photos.

- **Adhesive dots.** These dots are offered in different sizes and have a consistency similar to tacky, rubberized glue.

✓ **Sheets of adhesive.** You can cut these large double-sided adhesive sheets into different sizes and shapes.

✓ **Photo tape.** The tape comes on a roll and is a two-sided adhesive. You can cut the tape to the length(s) that you want.

✓ **Tape runners.** These dispense two-sided adhesive tape with a dispenser that you press and pull on the page.

✓ **Glue sticks.** The sticks dispense semi-solid adhesive in a push-up tube and are easy to use. Lots of people love to work with glue sticks.

✓ **Laminating adhesive machines.** You roll a flat item into this machine to get adhesive on one side and/or laminate on the other, or put laminate on one side and a magnet on the other.

Wet adhesives

You can find a variety of wet (liquid) glues that are "safe" for adhering photographs to your pages, but liquid adhesive can be tricky so we don't recommend using it for photos.

If you *do* use a liquid glue to adhere your photos, use it *very* sparingly. Remember that liquid glue is wet and too much of it can cause your photos to warp or make your pictures bubble.

Types of wet glue, sometimes preferred for adhering embellishments and accessories, include 2-way glue (in a squeezable container), 2-in-1 glue pen (with different sized push-down nib tips), metal glue (in a squeezable pen-like capped container), and spray adhesives that come in cans (use outdoors only).

Whatever you do, heed this advice . . .

Don't use adhesives on birth certificates, marriage licenses, or ultrasound printouts. Use mounting corners instead. And please don't laminate. The documents need to breathe, and laminate materials can bleed through into the emulsion on the paper.

Sticky situations

The definitions of *removable, repositionable,* or *permanent* adhesives aren't as straightforward as you may think. For example, some repositionable adhesives do become permanent after a while (the length of time this takes varies with different products).

When manufacturers say a product is repositionable, permanent, or removable, they're describing its qualities over the long term.

✔ **Removable:** If you want to be able to remove an adhered item without damaging it years from now (and the paper it's glued to), use a removable adhesive. EK Success and 3M both sell removable adhesive.

✔ **Repositionable:** These adhesives are like the adhesive on the back of a sticky note. You can move items around after you've adhered them to the page if you use repositionable adhesives. Great for beginning layouts — just use them within a limited time frame because some repositionables become permanent over time.

✔ **Permanent:** These adhesives join two items together — permanently, for the most part. Although you'll never use permanent adhesives for photos, you may use them for other materials. We recommend the permanent adhesives made by Magic Scraps, Tombow, Therm O Web, Xyron, 3L Corp, and 3M Scotch brand.

When you start out, be sure to choose a reversible, removable, or repositionable adhesive, rather than a permanent adhesive. Even experienced scrapbookers use *only* removable or repositionable adhesives for photographs.

Adding adhesives

At first, you'll probably adhere only photographs to your scrapbook pages. But soon you'll also want to glue things made of paper — like photo mats, journaling blocks, and die-cuts (see Chapter 6). We're also pretty sure that you'll start eyeing those popular 3-D embellishments (see Chapter 7). Here are some recommendations for adhering photos, paper, and 3-D embellishments to your pages.

- ✔ **Photos:** When you do put adhesive on the backs of photos, you want to use photo-mounting squares. Make sure that you buy squares made with *removable adhesives* so that you can "unstick" photos later, should you need to.

- ✔ **Paper:** Many scrapbookers use mounting squares or photo tape to glue items cut from thick and embossed papers (such as mats and journaling sheets). These adhesives are great for the thicker card stocks and printed papers: 2-way glue, glue sticks, vellum adhesives, and adhesive mounting squares.

- ✔ **3-D embellishments:** Embellishments are made from many different products, including metal, wood, clay, heavy-duty cardboard, glass beads, wooden beads, and wire. These adhesives will adhere your 3-D embellishments: Making Memories metal glue, scrappy glue, scrappy tape, glue dots, and Pop-Dots.

When using photo corners or photo pockets for mounting your photos, keep the following in mind:

- ✔ Photo corners stick onto the scrapbook page, not onto the photo. After measuring, adhere four photo corners onto the page and fit your photo into them. Some photo corners have to be dampened. Others come with a sticky adhesive and you just press them into place.

- ✔ Photo pockets and sleeves are like jackets for your photos. You can buy 3" x 5" photo pocket pages, adhere them to the pages, and then slide in your photos. You can also make your own photo pocket pages. Here's how: Cut a page protector to the size you want, adhere three of its sides to the page, and slip in your photo.

Any time you use an adhesive, decide first whether you want it to be removable (for photos), repositionable, or permanent. Keep the following information in mind when making your decision.

✔ **Read and follow the manufacturer's detailed directions to the letter.**

- If you're adhering items to pages made of special papers like mesh, handsewn, cloth, handmade, Diamond Dust, or printed or lush vellum papers, you should not only read the instructions, but you should also test the adhesive on your paper to make sure that it doesn't show through. (For vellums, we recommend using a tiny dot of Zig-2-way glue.)

- If you want more info than the manufacturer's directions give you, get help from your local scrapbook store. It pays to be sure that you have the right adhesives for adhering wood, newspaper clippings, clay, hair, cloth, ribbon, tags, or other materials you may have questions about. (For a complete listing of scrapbooking stores in the United States and to find the store nearest you, go to www.greatamericanscrapbook.com.)

✔ **Think thin!** Use small, small amounts of adhesive. Too much adhesive may ripple, bubble, or permanently damage the item you're adhering to the page.

Subtracting adhesives

Adding adhesives to your pages may give you more stick-to-itiveness than you bargained for. Maybe you've used too much glue and it's oozing onto your pages. Or maybe you don't want the adhesive where you thought you wanted it.

Fortunately, there are products that can remove many kinds of sticky stuff. *Un-Du* is one of the best — a great product for removing adhesive, stickers, or practically anything else you've stuck to your scrapbook page. Simply squeeze a few drops of the solution onto a scraper, slide the scraper underneath the object to be removed, and remove it. The adhesive will still be sticky, even after it dries.

Certainly, products that can get rid of unwanted adhesive are great. But it's easier to use the right adhesive in the first place. Opt for a repositionable or removable adhesive product, especially until you feel more confident about gluing. Later, you can move to using a permanent adhesive for your embellishments. But remember our advice (how could you forget it?) and always use a *removable* adhesive for your photos!

Before you buy your first adhesives

Stick-to-itiveness — important in all aspects of scrapbooking — is what adhesives are all about. Many scrapbook manufacturers have developed good acrylic-based adhesive products for sticking all kinds of stuff to scrapbook pages. The following adhesives checklist gives you an overview that can help you sort out what's what on all those adhesive shelves.

- ✔ **Avoid certain adhesives (as in *don't* use them in your precious scrapbooks).** Stay away from masking tape, duct tape, general office tape, rubber cement, or regular white craft glue (unless the label specifies that it's okay for scrapbooking projects).

- ✔ **Read the labels.** Carefully! Look for the words *photo safe, pH neutral, buffered,* and *non-hardening.* These terms indicate that the adhesives have been made to meet at least the minimum requirements of the scrapbook industry.

- ✔ **Read the disclaimers.** What *won't* the manufacturer guarantee? Be especially attentive to disclaimers when you're buying adhesives for adhering cloth, ribbon, plastic, buttons, metal, acrylic, beads, newspapers, and other "unusual" materials to your scrapbook pages.

- ✔ **Still Stuck?** Check out the manufacturers' Web sites (listed at Great American Scrapbook Company's Web site www.greatamericanscrapbook.com) or pick up your phone and call 800-3M-Helps. 3M will be happy to respond to your adhesive questions.

Page Protectors: A Saving Grace

Page protectors do the mighty job of protecting scrapbooks that will be thumbed through for years — maybe for generations. It's critical that the pages of these scrapbooks are protected from the natural oils on hands (big and small), from sticky fingers, accidental spills, tearing, dust, and scratches.

The hard-working page protector

We see page protectors as the workhorses of scrapbooking. Besides their primary job of protecting your pages, they're efficient little organizers and they don't even mind when you cut them up and turn them to any task your imagination can conjure up.

We put page protectors to work to help in the preliminary sorting out of our photos, memorabilia, and other items — while we're still in the process of figuring out what we want where (refer to Chapter 2).

Don't work your page protectors *too* hard. If you overstuff them, they may distort or become damaged.

Page protectors on overtime

Although you don't want to put too many items into your page protectors, you *can* work them overtime by transforming them into additions and extensions that give you more space for your scrapbook contents within the normal confines of standard albums.

Some manufacturers sew extenders onto the main page protectors. Others provide adhesive strips so that you can glue them on, and some come with the extenders already attached. Here are some "extenders" for your page protectors:

✔ **Simple page extenders:** Extenders attach to your page protectors' edges with an adhesive strip and can extend your pages from the top, bottom, or either side of the standard page protector.

✔ **Page flippers:** Flippers can be attached anywhere on top of your main page protector with a 2-way photo mounting adhesive. They measure 3" x 12" and can be trimmed to any size.

✔ **Panoramic spreads:** Panoramics give you four-page spreads, as shown in Figure 4-5, that fold out to the left and right of two facing pages in your album. Sewn together by the manufacturer, these page protector additions are used by many scrapbookers in place of the two-page spreads that have become so popular in recent years.

✔ **Peek-a-boo windows:** These little page protectors open like windows. You adhere them to the big page protector that's covering your scrapbook page. You can put more photos or journaling notes in these little peek-a-boos and attach them at different angles onto your big page protector.

✔ **Pop-up page protectors:** Pop-ups adhere to the inside corners of two facing scrapbook pages on the spine. They pop up when you open the two-page spread. (See Figure 4-6.)

✔ **Photo flips:** Flips are good for putting a lot of photographs onto one page in a compact space. These photo-sized page protectors flip over one another. Attach the photo flip strip to an existing full-sized page protector.

Photo courtesy of Ultra-PRO

Figure 4-5: A panoramic spread.

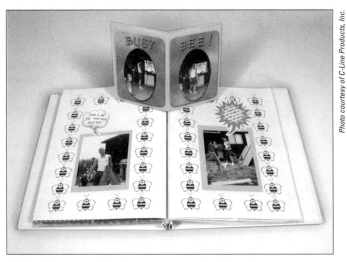

Photo courtesy of C-Line Products, Inc.

Figure 4-6: A pop-up page protector in action.

> ✔ **Quikits:** These come in 8½" x 11" and 12" x 12" sizes. The manufacturer has sewn little pockets onto the main page protector where you can put things like embellishments to keep them separate from your photographs. Put a 2-sided paper into your main page protector, use a complementary paper in the pockets, add your photos or embellishments, and you have a beautifully layered page.

> ✔ **Swing shutters:** Shutters adhere to the right and left edges of a main page protector. You can put items into the shutters, then close and open them over your page as you would open shutters over a window.

New technology: Polypropylene

For many years, most of the page protectors on the market were made of vinyl-based materials. In 1990, scrapbook manufacturer Ultra-PRO (formerly known as Rembrandt) launched a new technology — the polypropylene page. These page protectors were archival-safe, acid free, and had crystal-clear clarity. The polypropylene page protectors, an important addition to the scrapbooking industry, still have the highest clarity of any of the page protectors available today.

Purchasing page protectors

The plastic sleeves we call page protectors are such an integral part of scrapbooking that many manufacturers include them in the purchase price of their album systems. However, even if you buy an album that comes with page protectors, chances are good that you'll need more (*many* more), so you may as well add a few packages of page protectors to your scrapbook shopping list.

A page protector protects both sides of a scrapbook page. Like the albums, page protectors come in many sizes, from 4" x 5" to 12" x 15" and larger, as shown in Figure 4-7. Unlike albums (and adhesives for that matter), page protectors are relatively easy to shop for. The categories are simple and the options are limited: top-loading or side-loading; clear or non-glare; and polyethylene, polypropylene, or polyester (Mylar).

Photo courtesy of Ultra-PRO

Figure 4-7: A 12" x 12" sheet protector with the hologram safety seal.

We also tell you about some special types of page protectors. You may or may not want to experiment with these as you begin your experience with scrapbooking. Remember that you can always come back and check them out later if you think your plate is full enough for now.

✔ **Match your page protector to your album type and size.** Page protectors are made to fit into the standard post-bound albums, strap-hinge albums, or three-ring binders.

✔ **Top-loading or side-loading?** It's your call as to whether you choose page protectors that load from the top or the kind that load from the side. We like the side-loading type because we figure that dust can get into the pages from the top when the scrapbooks are stored on shelves.

✔ **Page-protector finishes.** We prefer a clear finish over a non-glare. But some people like the more subdued, almost cloudy look of the non-glare finishes. So again, the choice is yours.

✔ **Buy only in the 3P's category — the safe "polys"!**

- **Polyester or Mylar** page protectors are the Cadillacs of the page-protector market. Mylar is by far the best product to use for protecting your photographs, but the cost is very high ($10 for three 5" x 7" sleeves). Some high-end album systems come with Mylar page protectors. If you buy these, you'll probably be investing in Mylar refill protectors — as you'll want to get a consistent look.

- **Polypropylene** page protectors are used by a good percentage of scrapbookers. They run about $15 per 100 for 5" x 7" sleeves and sell like crazy because they're good quality and well priced at the same time.

- **Polyethylene** page protectors are safe for your photos and other scrapbook contents. At $10 per 100 for 5" x 7" sleeves, they're not expensive. These page protectors can be used as temporary "homes" for scrapbook contents when you're organizing and categorizing your scrapbook materials. And there's nothing wrong with using them for your finished albums.

Skip the magnetic album page protectors (even if they're labeled "acid-free"). These will destroy your photographs. And don't buy page protectors made with vinyl or acetate components! These components can stick to your photos, cause them to fade and change color, and ruin your scrapbook pages. Even if your photos aren't touching the vinyl, they're not safe.

If you know that you're going to want to include thick items in your scrapbooks (like room keys or dog tags), you can buy a package of embellishment page protectors. These protectors are stiffer than the standard sleeves, and many have protruding pockets that will go over your bulky items. These sleeves come in 8½" x 11" and 12" x 12" sizes. They not only prevent embellishment items from rubbing onto the opposite page, but they also protect the embellishments as well.

Now, you have your albums, the adhesive for your photos and memorabilia, and the protective sleeves for your pages. But don't head for the checkout counter quite yet! You still need cutting tools (see Chapter 5) and the papers that you'll transform into your unique scrapbook pages (see Chapter 6).

Page protectors as an art

Scrapbookers often use page protectors to make other things, such as envelopes, pocket pages, and *shaker boxes* (see-through square boxes that contain loose embellishment items).

✔ Your local scrapbook store will have a die-cut center where you can make die-cut envelopes out of page protectors. It's fun to use these see-through envelopes to enclose bright, cheery cards that you can send at holidays or just because you feel like it.

✔ You can make shaker boxes out of page protectors, too. Just cut a piece of the page protector out and attach the "box" with a two-way piece of adhesive to the page.

Chapter 5

Cutting-Edge Tools and Techniques

*S*crapbookers use cutting tools for all kinds of jobs. So naturally, the industry manufacturers have made hundreds of kinds of special tools for cutting paper, *cropping* (trimming) photographs, making mats and borders, snipping stickers, cutting dies, and performing many other cutting jobs as well.

In this chapter, we tell you about scissors and other cutting tools made for the scrapbook market. We also give you "need-to-knows" about how to use these products. And, of course, we include a handy shopping list, as well.

Cutting Tools and How to Use Them

The industry's hundreds of types of specialized cutting tools enable scrapbookers everywhere to work their magic. As you advance in scrapbooking, you're bound to become more familiar with the cutting tools we talk about in this section.

Although we tell you about our favorite cutting tools, be sure to experiment to find out which tools work best for you.

Scissor savvy

Scissors need a little pampering. Using your "paper-cutting" scissors for cutting other things (such as fabric, hair, and nails) dulls the blades. You can tell when scissors begin to dull because they seem to be tearing the paper as you cut. To help sharpen your scissors, cut some wax paper and/or aluminum foil. You can have them professionally sharpened, as well.

Scissors and scissor-cutting

Scissors are the simplest cutting tools for the beginning scrapbooker — and most people are already skilled in using them. Fiskars is one of the leading scissors brands in the scrapbook industry and makes more than 50 different scissors specifically for scrapbookers.

Once you know the kind of cutting task you have, pick the scissors that can best do the job from the wide variety of scissor types (see Figure 5-1).

Using the right pair of scissors for the job enables you to scrapbook along at a good clip.

Figure 5-1: Assortment of scrapbooking scissor types.

Basic scissor types

Here's a list of scissors you'll definitely want to have in your scrapbooking arsenal.

- ✔ **Straight scissors.** Straight-bladed scissors are measured from the tip of the blade to the bottom of the blade. Keep in mind that you can't use a five-inch pair of scissors for intricate detail cutting. For the control and precision you need, you want a small detail scissor to get into tiny corners.

- ✔ **Edgers.** Both decorative scissors and corner cutters are often referred to as *edgers,* which are rather versatile tools. By simply flipping the edger's blades around, you get another type of pattern. (Check out Figure 5-2 to see what a cut made by using a decorative edger looks like.)

When using decorative scissors, don't close the blades completely until you're ready for the final cut. Instead, cut only half way down the blade and then start another cut using the same tooth pattern. If you close the blades in the midst of cutting, the paper tears a little.

Figure 5-2: A border cut made by using a decorative edger.

- ✔ **Circle scissor.** The cutting part of this tool looks like a craft knife. The tool's plastic casing has little holes. You insert the cutting pen into these holes to make different-sized circles. You can make up to 125 sizes from 1" to 6" (see Figure 5-3). Using this tool is as simple as drawing something. You simply insert the blade vertically into the circle blade disc and gently press down to lock the blade in position. Reverse the blade direction to rotate in the opposite direction. When cutting, hold the swivel grip only tightly enough to allow the "pen" to rotate freely. Use less pressure when starting and stopping for the cleanest cuts.

Figure 5-3: Circle scissor at work.

Scissor techniques and tips

Doing a good cutting job requires concentration and focus. By keeping your eyes on what you're cutting and your scissors sharp, and by following these tips, you'll make successful cuts every time.

- ✔ As you're cutting paper, turn the paper instead of the scissors.

- ✔ Make long, continual cuts, not short little ones. Otherwise, you end up with jagged edges.

- ✔ Practice cutting a few pieces of scrap paper to get a good feel for the amount of pressure you need to make a good, clean cut.

- ✔ Draw a faint line in pencil on the item you're cutting. Cut just to the left or right of the drawn line.

- ✔ If you're using a pattern, replicate the pattern exactly and cut around the edges as carefully as possible.

- ✔ Measure twice. Cut once!

The blades of cutting tools are very sharp! Handle all blades carefully and keep them out of the reach of children.

Cutting — without using scissors

You can find so many incredible cutting tools on the market that we can't possibly tell you about all of them here. But, we do list, in alphabetical order, some of the most popular cutting tools that scrapbookers like to use. And, we give you a little information about what these tools are good for and how they work.

✔ **Circle cutter:** Makes cutting circles fast and easy. The sizes and mechanisms of circle cutters vary according to who makes them. Read the labels and be sure to use the mats recommended by the manufacturers.

✔ **Oval cutter:** Creates perfect ovals! — narrow and wide. *Carefully* follow the manufacturer's directions on the packaging. Be prepared to practice awhile to get the hang of this tool.

✔ **Paper trimmer:** Comes with different blades that change out easily (such as scoring blades, perforating blades, and various decorative blades). Trimmers are used for cropping your photos and paper and come in more than 20 different types and sizes. Some trimmers have a transparent finger guard, so that your fingers don't touch the photos or paper you're trimming. You can also find paper trimmers with swing-out rulers and with a paper guide to provide a level measuring surface (see Figure 5-4).

✔ **Rotary cutter:** Equipped with a long-lasting straight edge or decorative razor-sharp interchangeable blades. You *must* use a mat with this tool. Using a clear acrylic ruler when cutting straight edges is a good idea, as well. The contoured handle of the rotary cutter lets you simply roll along and enjoy cutting your edges, in a decorative or straight design.

✔ **Shape cutter:** Cuts just about any shape you want and cuts into paper and other materials, as well. The shape cutter has an adjustable blade depth, and is great for cropping and making border mats and for using with the shape templates (see the section "Cutting Shapes with Templates").

✔ **Swivel knife:** Uses a very small blade that rotates 360 degrees (see Figure 5-5). A swivel knife is good for cutting template shapes and for making small, intricate designs. You need a special foam mat when you use this knife (you'll damage the blade if you use a rubber mat). The blade steers itself, so you don't move your fingers or wrist. It's a lot like shifting gears in a car (the same movement) — just a simple pull of the arm will do.

Photo courtesy of Fiskars Brands, Inc.

Figure 5-4: A paper trimmer with a swing-out ruler and paper guide.

Photo courtesy of Provo Craft

Figure 5-5: A swivel knife is perfect for cutting out template patterns.

Cutting Shapes with Templates

Templates are patterns cut out of metal, brass, heavy card-stock, or simple plastic sheets (most often transparent). Scrapbookers use templates to create shapes out of papers and other materials.

Templates are inexpensive and easy to use. You simply trace a shape on the template and then cut on the traced line by using a swivel knife or other cutting tool.

You can use templates as patterns for cropping your photos by placing them over photos and cutting away the excess photo image. You also can use the templates to create frames to adhere to your pages, make mats for your photos, or cut out specifically shaped journaling blocks. Some translucent templates have a decorative edge that you can cut along with a shape-cutter tool. The edges have many designs and also have holes for easy storage in three ring binders.

Don't cut your only copy of an original photo. You can't undo what you've cut after you've cut it! Also, photo backgrounds usually tell a story, and the story may be one you don't want to lose.

Template systems

Most templates are sold individually, but many companies that make plastic templates include a cutting tool and a mat (and sometimes a replaceable blade) with the template. The tools and mats in these systems usually aren't interchangeable with similar systems offered by other companies.

- ✔ **EZ to cut:** This template-cutting system is terrific and makes creating complex-looking woven pages easy to do. Use two-toned cardstock for a dramatic look. Layer a contrasting color underneath for an entirely different look.

- ✔ **Coluzzle:** The templates in this system are unique. The channel widths on the templates are controlled so that a swivel knife can fit into the channel to cut perfect shapes time and time again. The Coluzzle system requires only the Easy Glide Cutting Mat.

Templates

The first templates in the scrapbook industry were simple shapes — circles, squares, and rectangles. Over time, templates have evolved into a large sector of their own, which has been incredible to witness. Now, templates come in all sorts of shapes and sizes and are often sold in theme groups (birthday, wedding, beach, baby, travel, garden, sports, vacation, camping, city, military, flowers, Aztec images, holidays, letters, and numbers, just to name a few!).

The swivel knife, described earlier in this chapter, is a good tool to use for cutting out shapes from almost all types of templates.

Working with specialty cutting templates

Specialty templates require certain, well, *special* stuff, like foam cutting mats, for example. The type of template you purchase will determine what kind of mat you need to buy. Just follow the manufacturer's directions. If you still have questions, talk with the independent scrapbook retailer nearest your home.

The old standard shapes (oval, circle, and square) are relatively easy to cut out, but other templates are complex and require cutting into tiny curves and corners.

Some templates have what are called *channels,* as shown in Figure 5-6. A channel is an open space on a template in which two pieces of plastic almost meet — in other words, the space in which you insert your knife as you cut around the edges of the pattern.

As you cut in the channel, you run into little plastic bridges (or webs). The webs help keep the template's shape in place, and also serve as a starting and stopping point for cutting.

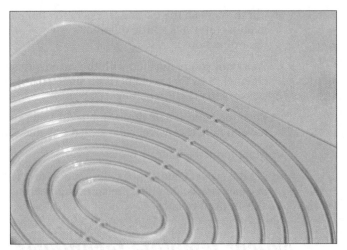

Figure 5-6: Illustration of channels and webs in a template.

Here are some tips to keep in mind as you cut a template:

✓ Hold the template firmly in place against the paper (or other material) you're cutting so that the template won't move.

✓ Always start a cut at the edge of the little plastic webs that hold the template shape together. Stop cutting when you get to the beginning of the next web. Then jump that web and continue cutting again on the other side. You don't want to cut or break the plastic webbing. If you do, the template falls into pieces.

Custom templates made by . . . you

As you get accustomed to working with templates, you may want to experiment with making templates of your own. You can create customized shapes and letters from any type of material — instantly. If you can cut the material, you can make a template from it. Heavy papers work well, but you can also try textured papers, thin metals, photographs, fabric, clay, and other materials.

✔ Cut through all the cutting tracks in the template (each manufacturer has a little different system — so review their directions).

Wait until you're finished with the cutouts to snip the channel webs that remain. Use a small pair of detail scissors to cut the webbing.

✔ Keep the knife at a 90-degree angle. In some systems, you have to hold the swivel knife straight up and down.

✔ Don't force the knife.

✔ Let the swivel knife — not your hand — do the twisting. In other words, don't tilt the knife handle from side to side or front to back.

No-cut template techniques

You may want to jazz up your template cutouts with some very fun new techniques.

While you have your templates out, take a break from cutting and try some of these fill-in tricks. They're fun, easy, and will give you wonderful results.

✔ **Inking:** Put ink right onto a wedge makeup sponge. Hold the template firmly on your paper and sponge the ink onto the open image within the template. Take away the template, and you have an inked image right on the paper.

Storing your templates

Templates are flat and light and store easily. Many templates come with three-ring holes so that you can store them in three-ring binders. If you store your templates loose, you can arrange them vertically or horizontally. But you never want to place objects under or on top of your templates. Handle templates carefully, avoid dropping them, and always keep them away from excessively hot or extremely cold temperatures.

✔ **Chalking:** Rather than coloring in the template shape with a pen, try using a cotton ball or a makeup wedge. Put chalk on the cotton or wedge and rub it into the open template shape. Hold down the template with one hand and apply the chalk with the other. You can also add ink for more variety and depth.

✔ **Metallic rub-ons:** Use these to add even more variety to your template shapes. Apply with a makeup wedge for a very artsy look that doesn't take a lot of time to create.

✔ **Stencil paste:** These templates let you create beautiful raised surfaces, as shown in Figure 5-7. Chalk under the template shape before filling in the shape with clear or milky stencil paste. The chalk will show through. Place the template on your paper or other material, hold in place, and smooth the stencil paste into the opening. Now you can sprinkle the paste with glitter or beads and create wild, colorful, and raised shapes on your page. Wait until the paste sets up to pull up the template. When you do, you'll have a little rough edge and a raised, clear shape or a milky-looking shape.

Photo courtesy of Fairy Tale Creations.

Figure 5-7: Making a raised surface template image with paste.

A Cutting-Tool Shopping List

The handful of cutting tools we recommend here is enough to get you through your first project. (As you become more experienced, you'll definitely want to experiment with some of the more specialized tools we tell you about.) Size and price ranges are wide, so focus on cutting tools you think you'd be comfortable using. Go with your instincts and select tools with a look and feel you like.

- ✔ **Sharp, straight-bladed scissors.** Buy two pair: one pair with relatively long blades for large-scale work and another pair with smaller blades for more intricate work. Make sure that the smaller pair has a micro tip, so that you can get into tiny corners.

- ✔ **Decoration-edged scissors.** These scissors cut borders around the edges of your pages and around the edges of the mats that frame your photos. Different blade shapes make different edges, such as scalloped, deckle, waves, and ripples, which are all popular choices.

- ✔ **Corner edgers.** These "oversized scissors" (in style types like art deco, corner rounder, and nostalgia) help give your scrapbook a professional look, as shown in Figure 5-8. You use these corner edgers to cut the corners of mats, photos, and papers.

Figure 5-8: This scrapbook paper is cut with a corner edger.

✔ **Exacto knife.** The knife's triangular blade is attached to a handle that you hold like a pen. The tip of the blade works great for picking up little things and the sharp, slanted blade is super for cutting straight lines in intricate areas. Always use a safety mat underneath the exacto.

✔ **Non-stick blades.** The *non-stick* label means that the blades are especially good for using when you're working with adhesives in your scrapbooks.

✔ **Handles.** Try a cutting tool's handles on for size and comfort. Lots of choices here: left-handed handles, right-handed handles, soft grip and soft touch handles, and so on.

✔ **Cutting mat.** A mat protects your work surface. Read cutting-tool labels for each manufacturer's recommendations about cutting mats.

✔ **Template rulers.** These are a real help when you want to create professional-looking borders and frames. You can draw along the lines with pen, chalk, or ink.

✔ **Templates.** Pick out some templates with patterns that go with the theme of the album you plan to make. Or just choose a few templates with images or shapes that suit your style (see "Cutting Shapes with Templates" later in this chapter for more about templates). Just cut out the shapes and adhere them to your pages.

Check cutting tools for sharpness. A sharp tool makes your job easier. (Any seasoned turkey-slicer will tell you the same thing).

Chapter 6

The Paper Trail

In This Chapter

▶ Making a list for the paper shopper

▶ Perusing paper types

▶ Using papers for pages, die-cuts, and punchies

*T*oday's creative scrapbookers use a lot of paper. Paper is the canvas on which they work, to which they stick things, and finally that which they tuck into page protectors for safekeeping.

When choosing paper, think about these three categories: color, size, and thickness. Decide which colors best express what you want your pages "to say" and what paper sizes and thicknesses you need for the album you plan to make.

In this chapter, we talk about the importance of the quality of paper that you buy. Quality paper is *PH neutral* (acid-free), *lignin-free* (no wood), and *buffered* (includes alkaline substances that neutralize any acids the paper may come in contact with). Yes, it's true that people sometimes do use paper that isn't archivally safe when making quick little projects, but we think that the effort you put into making *any* scrapbook justifies the purchase of quality materials.

Identifying Paper Types

The light-weight, solid-colored, and patterned papers are the paper types most used by scrapbookers. However, other kinds of paper have become increasingly popular in the current environment of experimentation, innovation, and artistic focus. Scrapbookers use different types of paper to serve different purposes within the same scrapbook.

✓ **Cardstock.** This heavy duty, thick-weight paper is good for using as a base, especially when you need a page that has to support embellishment items such as beads, metal items, buttons, and seashells. Cardstock is also great for paper piecing, journaling, paper weaving, crumpling, and many other projects (see the section, "Showing off with stylish paper tricks," later in this chapter for more about these terms). Use with patterned paper to add variety.

✓ **Corrugated.** Made from corrugated molds by DMD Industries, this heavy-weight corrugated paper comes in straight-line, wavy, and zigzag patterns.

✓ **Embossed.** Images are pressed into the back of one of these papers so that the images are raised on its front side (see Figure 6-1). Both K & Company and Lasting Impression sell beautiful embossed papers in many different patterns. We like to use embossed papers for frames and backgrounds.

✓ **Embroidered and sewn.** Provo Craft offers an embroidered specialty paper from India, as shown in Figure 6-2. Westrim also sells embroidered and sewn papers.

Don't cut embroidered or sewn paper because cutting may fray the paper's edges and the threads can eventually unravel.

✓ **Fabric.** "Fabric" paper is thick and lovely. Its textures give your pages a rich, full look and feel.

✓ **Handmade.** The softer colors and rough, natural textures of these papers make them popular for outdoor-photo pages and for *heritage albums.* Heritage albums are family albums created with old family pictures — usually black-and-white or *sepia* (brown-toned) photos. You can see the flower petals and natural fibers in the papers.

✓ **Metallic.** These papers are shiny, high-tech, and holographic. Two companies, New Dimensions Holographic Paper and Grafix, sell a lot of this paper — and make it available in many, many colors!

✓ **Mulberry.** This is a thin paper that looks heavier than it is because you can see so many of its fibers. Very versatile. You can tear the edges for a softening effect and to enhance the "natural" look of a page. Mulberry works as well for baby or wedding photos as it does for outdoors shots. Adds elegance to your pages.

Figure 6-1: The raised side of an embossed paper.

Figure 6-2: An embroidered specialty paper from India.

✔ **Parchment.** You can use parchment to achieve special effects. We've seen some beautiful scrapbooks in which scrapbook artists have used parchments to complement documents and memorabilia from earlier centuries.

✔ **Patterned.** The light-weight, patterned papers are as individual as the manufacturers who make them. Thousands of patterned papers exist on the market (we can't even count them because new ones are made every day).

✔ **Solid-colored papers.** Like patterned papers, these papers are generally light-weight. They're available in any color you can imagine (and some you can't!). Solid colors are great for mats, paper piecing, punching, crumpling, and complementing patterned and other kinds of papers.

✔ **Suede.** Many scrapbookers use suede papers for their heritage and wedding pages. The suedes, available in a wide array of colors, are nice for adding texture.

✔ **Vellum.** These rich, elegant papers are soft to the touch and easy on the eyes. Available in a variety of weights and beautiful colors, the vellums are often used for pocket pages, journaling with computer fonts, chalking, tearing, and crumpling. They look great layered, especially when you use different tones of one color (see Figure 6-3).

Photo courtesy of Ellison Craft and Design

Figure 6-3: A layered vellum page.

Creating Images Out of Paper

Obviously, you can do many scrapbooky things with paper besides just using it for standard album pages. In this section, we tell you about some awesome paper techniques and then explain how paper is used with die-cut machines and paper punches.

Showing off with stylish paper tricks

These techniques may take a little extra time to master, but the results look mighty impressive on the page. Crumpling is probably the easiest trick to pull off, and paper folding the most difficult. If you like "oohs" and "aahs," give these a try.

- **Color blocking:** Cut colored papers to equal sizes and put them together to create a mosaic-like look.

- **Crumpling:** Makes you feel like a kid again. Wet a whole piece of paper with a spray bottle. Crumple the paper, then open it and crumple it again to give the paper an old, leathery look. The process shrinks the paper a little bit, so factor in the shrinkage. If you're going to do a border, allow for the shrinkage so that the border will cross the entire edge of the page.

- **Paper folding:** Is a lot like *origami* (the Japanese art of folding paper to create figures and designs). Manipulate the paper into various forms. Many idea books on the market show you in-depth techniques on how to make everything from little pinwheels to tiny paper T-shirts.

- **Paper piecing:** Cut shapes out of paper and piece them together to form an image. You can buy all kinds of paper-piecing patterns or make your own. This piecing technique adds dimension and variety to your page.

- **Paper tearing:** Fun and easy to do. When you want the fibrous part of the tear to show on your page (and you will!), hold the paper in your fingers and tear the paper toward you.

Lightly wetting the paper along the line you want to tear will make the tearing easier — a good trick, especially with Mulberry paper.

Paper die-cuts

Dies are a little like cookie cutters that come in different shapes and sizes. *Die-cutting machines* are usually made out of metal, although some are constructed of heavy-duty plastic. In scrap-booking, the *die-cuts* are the paper "cookies" (unbaked of course and totally without calories) cut out by the dies.

No scissors needed. Die-cuts give you a fast and easy way to embellish your pages with shapes cut from paper.

Die-cuts made from paper are very popular with scrapbook-ers. (And, these days precut die-cuts made out of metal, fabric, clay, and other materials are also becoming popular as embellishments.)

Packaged die-cuts

You can buy precut die-cuts in packages. These paper "cutouts" come cluster-packaged in every shape, color, and theme imag-inable. Many laser die-cuts are also available on the market, many of which are amazingly intricate and delicate (see Fig-ure 6-4).

- ✔ **Pre-packaged die-cuts.** The die-cuts in these packages usually come in solid colors only, often feature a theme, and can be flipped over if needed — you can, for exam-ple, make your arrow die-cut point in the opposite direc-tion just by flipping it over. If you're making a beach page, you can buy a die-cut package that includes waves, a beach ball, a sun, and the other things that go with a beach theme.

- ✔ **Pre-printed die-cuts.** Photographic images, made from various grades and weights of paper, are printed right on these individual die-cuts (usually four-color images). The image, printed on one side of the die-cut only, can look like the real thing. (We've seen cookie die-cuts that look good enough to eat.) Occasionally, you see these loose die-cuts with a white edge around them. Just trim off the edge with your detail scissors.

- ✔ **Laser die-cuts.** These die-cuts are sold in packages or individually. They're addicting — and we're not going to confess how many we have in our studios.

Photo courtesy of Ellison Craft and Design

Figure 6-4: Intricate laser die-cuts.

Die-cutting machines

Die-cutting machines cut shapes (die-cuts) by means of the sharp metal shapes attached to the bottom of wooden dies (these metal shapes are called *steel-rule dies*). The dies are placed into the press or rolled through the die-cutting machine.

A repurposing of industrial dies . . .

Die-cutting has been around for a long time in the industrial sector (though not necessarily appreciated). In the scrapbook world, die-cuts have come into their own and are admired and appreciated not just by scrapbook artists, but by those who view their work as well.

Obviously, you can't fit an expensive, industrial die-cutting machine into your scrapbook supply bag! These machines, as shown in Figure 6-5, have to stay put because of their weight. You can, though, use these heavy-duty machines at many scrapbook retail stores if you know where to go. Or, you can buy a smaller, personal die-cut machine.

✔ **Die-cut centers.** You can find an industrial die-cut machine at any well-stocked scrapbook store. Each store has its own policy, but usually, you pay by the hour to use the machine. Sometimes, if you buy the store's paper, they won't charge you for using their die-cut machine. More than 6,000 different die types are available to choose and cut from, and the big machines can usually cut more than one piece of paper at a time. (You can also use the dies to cut light craft-metal, fabric, household sponge, fun foam, static vinyl, mat board, laminate papers, and many other materials.)

✔ **Personal systems.** Personal die-cutting systems are becoming more common. These systems are great for home use, and you can carry the new smaller die-cut systems with you when you go to a scrapbook convention or to a friend's house to crop.

- QuickCuts makes a portable personal die-cut system that weighs less than 2 pounds. It's compact enough to fit in your handbag.

- Ellison and Provo Craft teamed up to make a personal die-cut machine that's called the Sizzix. The machine weighs about 13 pounds and sells for $79.99.

- AccuCut's personal die-cut Mini Machine costs $150 and weighs 10 pounds. It can accommodate and is compatible with all other commercial dies.

- Zip'e Mate by Dayco retails for $129.99. Although the system weighs only 7 pounds, it has the industrial strength of the big die machines. Made with solid aluminum rollers, Zip'e Mate can accommodate a 5" wide die and can also use dies made by other companies.

Photo courtesy of AccuCut Systems, Dayco, Zip'e Enterprises, Inc., and Ellison Craft and Design

Figure 6-5: A grouping of industrial die-cut machines.

Tapping into die-cut techniques

Whether you want to use die-cuts for lettering, framing, or accenting your page theme, you can be sure that you'll find one or more of these little cutouts that helps you "tell the story." Have fun with them. They're versatile, and they help make your scrapbooking experience simple yet rewarding.

- ✔ **Chalking on paper die-cuts.** Adds depth to your page. You can use a cotton swab, an eye-makeup sponge applicator with a handle, or the applicator that comes with the chalk to apply the chalk to the edges of the die-cut and rub it in. Then do some *stitching* with a fine-point black pen by making little black marks that look like stitches.

- ✔ **Die-cuts as frames.** You can use frame die-cuts for your photos. Just *crop* (trim) the photo to fit inside the die-cut frame (see Figure 6-6).

- ✔ **Embellished die-cuts.** Simply decorate a die-cut with glitter, beads, fibers, paints, chalks, or whatever else you want to use. Voilà! You have an embellished die-cut.

✔ **Journaling.** You can write on the die-cuts that you adhere to your scrapbook pages. The die-cut itself adds meaning to the little story you write on it.

✔ **Layered die-cuts.** Using the same die, such as a sunflower, cut out two or more colors to create a layered image. Use one die to cut three identical shapes — in green, yellow, and black. Use the green for the flower stem, place the yellow sunflower on top of it, and then put the black in the center of the flower.

✔ **Letters.** Every company offers its own variations of die-cut letters and letter systems — alphabets in a tremendous variety of styles. These die-cuts are used for titles and other lettering tasks. You can put shadows behind them by cutting out the same letter in a contrasting color. Or, you can use a solid die-cut block behind the letter.

Photo courtesy of Ellison Craft and Design

Figure 6-6: A sunflower die-cut framing a photo.

Pulling no (paper) punches

The paper shapes that scrapbookers cut out with punches are affectionately known as *punchies*. The punches that cut the paper are *sort of* like die machines, but much smaller. Often referred to as "craft punches," these punches are powerful little tools. They're plastic on the outside, but their intricate innards are made with steel.

Punches are available in many sizes — from 2¼" down to 1". Punches also come in many different styles and patterns. We use them to make punchies out of our leftover paper.

Punches are versatile. The basic shapes (circles, squares, and a corner rounder) are *must-haves.* You can build and layer to your heart's content with these shapes (see Figure 6-7). But you'll probably also want to look at some of the holiday and other categories of punches.

Photo courtesy of Ellison Craft and Design

Figure 6-7: A title made with die-cuts on punchie squares.

If you pack a punch, keep it sharp!

You can use aluminum foil to sharpen your punches, and you can lubricate them with waxed paper. If your punches start to make rough cuts, cut all the way through the foil two or three times. If a punch seems to be sticking, use the punch on wax paper and it should be good as new.

To create a punchie, place your paper in the little slit on the punch and push down on the punch "button." There's your shape. (See Figure 6-8).

Figure 6-8: Making a Christmas tree punchie.

Here are some things to keep in mind when working with punchies.

- ✔ Use a pair of tweezers when you work with small punched shapes. The tweezers will help you keep your work area cleaner, and you'll have less glue mess.

- ✔ Use Squeeze & Roll adhesive. It's the best adhesive for adhering small punched pieces. You can put a pinhead-sized drop (no more!) on the back of your punched shape and press the punchie into place on the page.

- ✔ When gluing punched pieces, place the adhesive on the largest piece (the foundation) of the punch art first. Then adhere the smaller punched pieces on top of the first piece.

Buying Paper: Your Shopper's Guide

Paper comes in hundreds of textures, types, and colors. (For more about colors and how to choose them, refer to Chapter 3.)

Paper is sold in shrink-wrapped packages, in books of paper, and as single sheets. You can buy sheets of paper with different colors and patterns on each side. You can buy two-tone papers. You can even buy . . . well, you'll see, but before you do, take a look at these shopping tips.

- ✔ **Read labels.** Look for these words: *PH neutral* or *neutral, buffered, lignin-free,* and *acid-free.* The more you see these words on the label, the better.

- ✔ **Buy more sheets than you think you need.** Buy extras (at least ten more sheets than you think you need) because Murphy's law never fails here. When you're sure that you have enough paper, you don't — which quickly becomes obvious when you're working on your project. Also, with scrapbooking, the advice about buying papers from one *dye lot* (the set amount of paper in one run, printed at one time) is the same as it is with wallpaper. The inks that dye the paper can vary slightly on each separate run, and you want a uniform dye for each color you pick.

✔ **Select a variety of papers.** Trying a few different sizes and types of paper will inspire you as you begin to work. DieCuts with a View sells small mat stacks (4½" x 6½" to 5½" x 7½"); Bazzill Basics Paper Company offers many cut papers (from 4" x 12" to 12" x 12"); Canson, Inc., imports beautiful high-quality paper from France (sizes 8½" x 11" to 19" x 25"); Prism Papers is known for its colors (over 500 of them); and Paper Adventures is known for its leading-edge designs — check out their quadrant line.

✔ **Take a color wheel.** By having a color wheel (and a few of your main photos) with you when you shop, you can make sure that all the embellishments and stickers match or complement your paper selections.

Storing your papers

Storing papers in a home environment is the best method. Keep your papers out of direct sunlight and away from humidity. Store them flat and, if possible, organize your paper collection in the same sequence as the color wheel, which is R (Red), O (Orange), Y (Yellow), G (Green), B (Blue), I (Indigo), and V (Violet): "ROYGBIV" (for more on color, refer to Chapter 3).

Chapter 7

Accessorize!

- -

In This Chapter

▶ Surveying stickers, stamps, templates, coloring tools, and embellishments

▶ Skimming the shopping lists

▶ Tips and techniques for accenting your pages with accessories

- -

*A*fter working with photographs and papers to create an album, you may get an urge to dress up your pages with accessories. Like wardrobe accessories, *scrapbook accessories,* or extras, reflect individual style and taste. And just as belts, scarves, and jewelry can "make the outfit," stickers, stamps, and coloring tools can turn a good-looking page into a real stunner.

This chapter highlights the tried, true, and trendy in scrapbooking accessories: classic stickers and new ways to use them, stamps and templates, pens and other magical coloring tools, and embellishments — the hot new fad in scrapbooking.

Scoping Out the Stickers

A *sticker* consists of an image (or a pattern) and an adhesive. The images on stickers are copied from photos and various kinds of art. Manufacturers adhere stickers to *sticker liners* and sell the stickers on sheets, rolls, and individually. A single company often produces over a thousand different sticker designs. (For more on sticker liners, see the sidebar, "What's a sticker liner, anyway?")

What's a sticker liner, anyway?

Sticker liners are the plasticized sheets that your stickers are adhered to when you buy them. You can peel the stickers off the sticker-liner surface and put them back on again (as often as you like) without compromising the sticker's adhesive.

 Stickers are usually made out of paper (like postage stamps), but you can also find vellum paper, felt, fabric, and other specialty stickers in the scrapbook stores.

Situating stickers

Photographs are the focal points of scrapbook albums. The unadorned photo, like an unadorned person, is certainly interesting enough on its own. But you can make that photo even more interesting by contextualizing it within a design. When carefully placed, stickers do just that by becoming useful elements in your overall page design.

 Before you start sticking stickers here, there, and everywhere, refer to Chapter 3 for a quick review of design principles.

Your sticker strategies can help you achieve a pleasing composition, *depth of field* (perspective), and balance on the page.

Composition

Very simply put, composition is about how the shapes and images on a canvas are placed in relation to each other. Your goal is to create a pleasing arrangement.

Here's how:

- ✔ Cut the stickers you plan to use out of the sticker liner, but leave the liner backing on.

- ✔ Compose your page by moving the loose stickers around to look at the different ways you might place them. Arrange the stickers with all of your page items (photos and other accessories) until you get the placement you want. Then, peel off the liner and adhere the stickers to the page.

Perspective

Here are various ways that you can add dimension and depth to your page.

✔ Placing your biggest stickers near the bottom of the page with smaller stickers closer to the top adds perspective. For example, if you want to create an image of a pathway that suggests distance, put flowers on either side of the path — big ones toward the bottom, smaller ones in the middle, and still smaller ones toward the top of the page.

✔ Overlapping is another way to add depth and perspective to your page (see Figure 7-1). Place stickers on top of each other so that they overlap. Put the background stickers down first and overlap the other stickers on top of one another toward the bottom of the page.

Put tree stickers (big or small) on the bottom of the page. Otherwise, they look like they're floating in air.

✔ Layer stickers onto strips of colored paper. Place the stickers you want to appear the farthest away toward the top of the page and stickers you want to appear closer toward the bottom.

Photo courtesy of Mrs. Grossman's Paper Co.

Figure 7-1: This overlapping technique creates the illusion of depth.

Balance

Balance is about how things are weighted on a page. Size and color are the elements that determine a viewer's perception of weight. Black is heavy. Big is heavy. Putting this combination together is *very* heavy. To create a pleasing balance on a page, equalize the weight, or match things — by putting two images of the same flower on either side of a path, for example.

If you want to create certain special effects, vary the weight according to the message you want to transmit.

- ✔ Cluster stickers, rather than putting individual stickers "any old place." Doing so can help to create balance.

- ✔ Use border stickers to balance a page. Put these long, narrow strips of variously designed stickers around the four corners of your pages, around your matted photos, or around an entire page (see Figure 7-2).

Figure 7-2: Border stickers balance a spread.

Store your stickers just like you store your albums — away from heat and humidity and in the most temperate part of your home. If you improperly store the album itself, the stickers in your finished albums can get gooey and/or lose their stickiness.

Sticker techniques

Should you decide to try any of these sticker techniques, remember one overarching principle: Easy does it! When you first put a sticker on a page, put it down lightly. After you know for sure where you want it, *burnish* the sticker onto the page by placing a piece of paper over the sticker and rubbing the sticker onto the page.

Here are some great ways to use stickers:

✓ **Cropping:** You can cut and rearrange the parts of a sticker to add a sense of action to your page, as shown in Figure 7-3. Use your straight-edge scissors or a craft knife and a mat to crop (cut and/or trim) the sticker.

✓ **Pop ups:** Make a sticker "pop" off the page by adhering a "Pop-Dot" adhesive to the back of the sticker. Use a small brush to powder the sticky side of the sticker. Doing this gets rid of its adhesive. Use the "Pop-Dot" to adhere the sticker to the page.

 Stickers are friendly icons, and they make people smile. But watch out! Kids love these things and will stick them on any and all available surfaces — including your walls and floors.

✓ **Sticker scenes:** Try using stickers to make little scenes on your scrapbook pages (mountains, clouds, trees, rivers, animals, or anything you like). Many manufacturers offer stickers that mirror each other so that you can manipulate direction when you want to.

✓ **Photo mats and frames:** Create little frames for your photographs with a series of stickers.

 Don't put stickers directly *on* your photos because the photo emulsion may have an adverse reaction to the sticker adhesive over time.

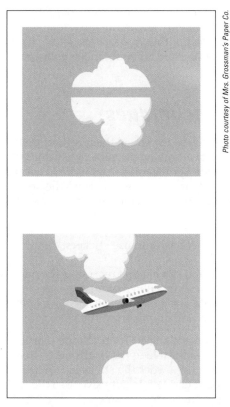

Figure 7-3: Cut and rearrange stickers to add a sense of action.

Sticker shopping

When you go sticker shopping, you can avoid the temptations lurking in sticker land by choosing only stickers that go well with your themes, papers, photos, and albums.

Here are some sticker tips to keep in mind as you buy:

- ✔ **Choose die-cut sticker images** with sharp, clean-cut edges rather than sticker images printed on a white background — then you won't have to spend time cutting off the white edges around the sticker image.

Buying stickers made by the same manufacturer helps you achieve unity and consistency in an album.

✔ **Stick with the "sticker art" you like** — choose stickers that reflect your style — in the same way you choose home décor, fashion, and food items.

✔ **Pick up a good pair of tweezers** for lifting stickers and placing them on your pages.

✔ **Get a pair of straight scissors** with coated blades. The coating resists the adhesive buildup that comes from cutting out lots of stickers.

✔ **Buy a "Little Chizler"** tool for getting under and removing those stickers you've stuck on a page and then decided you didn't want there after all.

✔ **Check out Un-Du,** which works well for removing stickers without damaging the stickers or the paper.

✔ **Find a sticker binder system,** like the one shown in Figure 7-4, that organizes your stickers with page protectors.

Figure 7-4: A sticker binder lets you view your sticker stash at a glance.

Attention: Sticker-happy shoppers . . .

Buying large quantities of stickers for no reason other than you just plain love them? Okay then. Consider yourself stuck on stickers. When you end up collecting stickers (as we do), you need a storage, accessibility, and inventory-rotation plan: Store your extra stickers in a readily accessible place, and *use* them frequently on cards, envelopes, and other things besides your scrapbook pages.

 If you want to try some of the sticker techniques in this chapter, you need the following items: metal ruler, craft knife, stylus (marking device), inscribing pen for metal tags, mat, adhesive (foam squares, dots, and/or mounting tape), powder (such as baby or talcum; cornstarch also works), and a small paint brush for applying the powder.

Searching for Stamps

If you have an artistic flair, you'll definitely have fun working with stamps. Stamps are simple to use. Just ink the stamp's rubber design with ink from an inkpad and press the stamp's image or pattern onto your page.

Stamping tips and techniques

Scrapbooking stamps, unlike stickers, can be used over and over again to create images on a page. Stamps add a personal touch, plus design and color variety, to your pages.

Here's how:

- ✔ **Creating patterned papers:** You can stamp your scrapbook pages with any kind of stamp to make repeating patterns in various colors. Use images, swirls, or any other stamp design you like.

- ✔ **Short journaling:** Use your word, number, alphabet, and symbol stamps to make page titles, photo captions, photo corners, borders, and whatever else you can think up.

✔ **Designing:** The thousands of stamp images created by the scrapbook industry's manufacturers translate into a designer's paradise. You can incorporate any stamped image (in any color) into your layout design.

Be sure to keep the following tips in mind when working with stamps:

✔ Don't use soap and water to clean your stamps. Clean them with a commercial stamp cleaner, or just stamp them a few times on a damp paper towel and then clean the stamp with baby wipes (they have a built-in conditioner).

✔ Before using a new stamp on an album page, practice stamping it on scratch paper so that you know how much ink to use and how much pressure to apply when you stamp it.

✔ When stamping, don't rock the stamp back and forth. Apply the same pressure all the way across the stamp and lift the stamp straight up so that you don't smudge your page.

Trying Out Templates

Scrapbookers use templates in a lot of different ways. (Refer to Chapter 5 for more about templates.) Templates can help you create some beautiful accessories for your albums. You can use plastic templates to make accessories, or you can use the brass embossing templates.

Many methods for transferring a template image onto the scrapbook page exist. *Sponging* and *embossing* (raising an image from the paper's flat surface) are two techniques — and they produce really interesting results.

✔ **Sponging:** To sponge on color using a template, dab your sponge onto a pigment-based ink pad. Test on scratch paper. Then sponge the color softly onto the open sections of the template you've laid on your page.

✔ **Embossing:** To emboss, you use a template and raise the image from the page by using a *stylus,* which is a metal, pen-like instrument with a different-sized metal ball on each end for pressing along the edges of the template's image. You can dry emboss or use heat, as follows.

To dry emboss with a template, follow these steps:

1. **Using a brass template, place the template on the plastic top of a *light box* (a box with a light in it).**

   Note: You can use any light source, such as a window.

2. **Lay your paper on top of the template.**

3. **Gently trace the outline of the template design with your stylus.**

   The stylus pushes the paper out

4. **When you're through tracing, turn the paper over and you'll see the raised image.**

   You can decorate the embossed area by sponging, adding glitter, or coloring the area with pencils or markers.

To emboss with heat using a template, do this:

1. **Lay a brass template on a page.**

2. **Dab the open design on the template with a pigment or embossing ink.**

3. **Remove the template and sprinkle embossing powder (clear, colored, or metallic) over the inked area.**

4. **Tap off the excess powder.**

5. **Heat the powder with an embossing gun (don't use a blow dryer — it won't work).**

   You now have a raised image on your page.

Shopping for stamps and templates

As is the case with most scrapbooking materials, stamps come in tons of shapes, sizes, designs, and themes. The scrapbook industry's pigment inks (used in stamping pads) are extremely long-lived. Another plus — the colors of the ink stay true!

A lowly stamp's noble lineage?

The scrapbook stamp may trace its ancestry to the seals used by kings, nobles, and others who impressed an identifying image onto a surface by stamping it into hot wax — thus "sealing" their communiqués.

Shopping for stamps and templates means shopping for the images, words, and designs you think will work well with your scrapbook designs. Both stamps and templates are good bargains because you use them over and over again.

- ✔ **Alphabet and word stamps** are popular for making titles, borders, words, captions, headings, and short journalings. You more than get your money's worth with an alphabet stamp set.

- ✔ **Wood or acrylic-mounted stamps** are better than the less expensive foam-mounted stamps.

- ✔ **Stamp pads** are available in as many ink colors as you think you can use — the best stamp pads are made with pigment-based inks. Buy these instead of die-ink pads.

- ✔ **Assorted templates** are available to use for special techniques like sponging and embossing. Be sure to get brass templates and a stylus if you plan to do any embossing.

Store your stamps face down — keep them away from sun and high temperatures.

Using Writing and Coloring Tools to Archive

Writing and coloring tools *can* be weak links in the chain of archival materials. Inks are the culprits, not the tools themselves. Inks that will last for 100+ years are pigment-based. They're waterproof, *fade resistant* (won't fade on your pages), and *light fast* (they won't "disappear" even when exposed to light over extended periods).

Inks are an issue even when you're using a computer to journal. Inkjet printer ink will not last as long as a pigment-based ink. Pigment based inks are a little more expensive, but not exorbitant.

Forensic scientists, archaeologists, anthropologists, museum preservationists, cartoonists — and others who really value archival standards — take care not to create weak links with bad inks.

Working with pens, markers, colored pencils, and chalks

Pens reveal the character of your writing, whereas markers tend to obscure it (markers mask the little idiosyncrasies that make your handwriting unique). The thinner pen point transfers your personality directly onto the scrapbook page and adds to the value of your album. (Your great grandfather's e-mail message doesn't impart the same meaning as the note he wrote with a frail and shaking hand.)

Pens

Pens are better for scrapbook journaling than markers — and not just any old pen. You need to use a journaling pen, one that meets industry standards by having pigment-based ink.

The important differences in pens aren't in the barrels of the instruments. The ink, not the pen itself, is what's left behind — and the ink is what's important. No one will care what the barrel looked like 100 years from now. The writing you do in your album with a Sakura Pigma Micron pen will last longer than the paper in the album. (See Figure 7-5 for a variety of Sakura's journaling pens.)

Even if you're using the finest pens and inks, what you write may look like Hieroglyphics to your ancestors if you don't take a little extra care with your penmanship.

Keep your pens in a drawer or storage organizer so that you can lay them flat. Be sure to keep their lids on tight so that the inks don't dry out.

Photo courtesy of Sakura Pigma Micron

Figure 7-5: An assortment of journaling pens.

Markers, colored pencils, and chalk

Markers, colored pencils, and chalk are used more for color and design than for journaling, although using markers and colored pencils for short phrases and titles is sometimes effective in adding a splash of variety to a page.

- ✔ **Markers and colored pencils** are good for outlining stamped or other kinds of lettering. Scrapbookers use colored pencils for blending and shading colors and for adding specific details to a page. You can lighten and darken colors by using different pressures.

- ✔ **Chalk** is a compressed, powdered colorant. Its main purpose in scrapbooking is to make items on the page stand out. Scrapbookers frequently chalk the edges of die-cuts and the edges of album pages to draw attention to the borders. You can also use chalk to make backgrounds for your pages or to create focal points. Chalk works well on rough textures because it sticks in the texture fibers and crevices. The rougher the paper, the better the chalking looks.

Shopping for writing and coloring tools

The artistes of the scrapbook world (refer to Chapter 1) have a special affinity for writing and coloring tools. They make beautiful designs and images with these tools. Some of their work looks like the finest of fine art. And the integration of their photos onto these pages isn't intrusive, but rather an interesting blend of the realistic photo image and the art they've created.

Try your hand with these tools a little at a time. You can begin by adding a touch of color here and there. These items will give you plenty of incentive to get started.

- ✔ **Primary and secondary colors** are your best bets when you first shop for writing and coloring tools.

- ✔ **Markers or paint pens in white, black, gold, and silver** — do buy one each of these pens to create dramatic highlights.

- ✔ **Brand names,** like American Pen, EK Success, Marvey Uchida, Sakura of America, and Staedtler ensure that you get the best inks.

- ✔ **Pigment-based inks** are *the* best of the inks, bar none. Metallic-based inks, for example, don't last nearly as long, and the alcohol-based inks dry out and fade over time.

- ✔ **A package of assorted pen nibs** that come in lots of sizes, as shown in Figure 7-6. You'll find your favorites after you experiment for a while.

- ✔ **Gelly roll pens** come in a variety of colors — the first five colors of the gelly roll (black, blue, red, green, and purple) are pigment-based.

- ✔ **A set of chalks** — you can buy sets of pastel or of primary colors. Some manufacturers make an assortment set that mixes the pastels and the primaries.

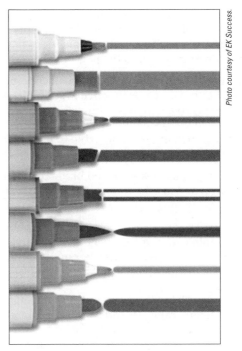

Photo courtesy of EK Success.

Figure 7-6: An assortment of decorative markers.

Embellishments: The New Rage

If you like high fashion, you'll love the embellishment part of scrapbooking. An *embellishment* is an adornment. Put embellishments on your pages, and you automatically bump your layouts up a notch.

Embellishments are inexpensive, easy to use, and make great design elements. Currently, the most popular embellishments are made of metals.

Here's a list of different types of metal embellishments:

- **Eyelets (also called grommets):** Come in all sorts of sizes, colors, and designs (one company has 250 grommet designs). Eyelets are made of either aluminum or brass (the brass have a lot more detail than the aluminum, but the aluminum is softer).

Eyelets are often chosen for their symbolic relationship to the theme of a page. For example, a scrapbooker telling a story about a trip to a museum's gardens might incorporate flower eyelets into the page layout.

Buy an eyelet setter and a wooden mallet before you set an eyelet into your page. Practice first on scrap paper. The best way to avoid oversetting an eyelet is to use a light-weight (8 oz.) wooden mallet. A mallet is a lot easier to use and much more comfortable to hold than a metal hammer.

✓ **Brads:** You can use two-pronged brads to adhere items to the page, and in other innovative ways, like using them to make metal images such as flowers made out of brads.

✓ **Metal tags:** These can add (inexpensive) pizzazz to your page. Scrapbookers write dates on them with a little metal inscriber, or they use the inscriber on them to replicate dog tags on military pages.

Scrapbookers use all kinds of materials for embellishments: wire, ribbons, hemp, raffia, threads, little beads and sequins, seashells, buttons. This field is wide open!

Part III
The Part of Tens

The 5th Wave   By Rich Tennant

"I'd like to take up scrapbooking. I'm just not sure I have that much whimsy in me."

In this part . . .

We persuade you that in scrapbooking, journaling is right up there in importance with your photographs. We invite you to try ten of the most interesting of the journaling techniques — we know that if you do, you're sure to find one or more journaling methods you really *like* to use.

If you somehow still aren't convinced that journaling is for you, use the top scrapbooking idea Web sites to look up what others have said about scrapbook journaling. Get ideas from retailers and manufacturers, from scrappers in the chat rooms, or get advice from an online Q & A about how you too can get enthused about writing for your scrapbook pages. These Web sites are all worth visiting — for info about journaling, and for practically anything else about scrapbooking that you find intriguing.

Chapter 8

Ten Ways to Journal in Your Scrapbook

In This Chapter

▶ Writing around the edges of your pages

▶ Using your calendar as your muse

▶ Getting the knack of tinkering with building blocks

▶ Putting secrets away in page protectors

*H*ey! Why bother journaling when the photos already tell the story? Well, here are but a few of the reasons why journaling is worthwhile:

✔ Your photos won't tell the *whole* story — (who the heck *are* those people with Uncle Walter????).

✔ Your memory may be gone before you are.

✔ Journaling is better for your credit rating than power shopping.

✔ You'll improve your handwriting.

Okay, now that we're serious about getting down to the business of journaling, here are ten simple ways to incorporate journaling into your scrapbook pages. In no time, you'll be spilling the family beans.

The who/what/when/where/why + the heartaches + the thank yous = a fantastic history for posterity.

When you journal, write on one side of the paper only. Ink can bleed through paper over the years and make your words illegible.

Storytelling, the Alphabet and Word Stamp(s) Way

At a loss for words? Use alphabet and/or word stamps to tell your story. Single-word stamps (*Oops! Wow!! Courage!*) are great for capturing the essence of what you want to say. Listing seven or eight words on the page can create a powerful effect. Use a uniform style or mix up the letter sizes for an uneven, jumbled look, and be sure to stamp boldly!

If you have a lot to say, stamping it out one thump at a time isn't very practical.

Traveling around the Border

Border journaling makes your page interactive. Readers have to turn your album upside-down and sideways to see what you've written. Start on a corner of the page and continue writing around the entire border (you determine how wide you want the border to be). If you journal around the border of a two-page spread, don't write in the *gutter* — where the two pages meet (no one wants to read gutter prose).

Borrowing from Your Calendar Entries

Try calendar journaling. Post a personal or family calendar on the fridge. Keep notes on what's happening *when* it happens. Later, you can either transfer your notes onto a pre-made scrapbook calendar page, use the calendar itself in your album, or just use it as a journaling guide when you're making your pages.

Putting Your Computer to Work

Use any computer word program you like to say what you want to say. Print your text on a colored or patterned paper, then cut the paper into a shape and adhere it to your scrapbook page.

Contact the company that made your color printer and ask whether the ink is pigment-based (best) or die-based (doesn't last as long).

Getting Crafty with Die-Cuts

Scrapbookers often use die-cuts symbolically to reinforce themes or ideas on a page. If you're doing a garden page, journal on a rototiller die-cut about preparing the soil and write about the planting on a seed package die-cut. Use flower and plant die-cuts to describe the garden, and write about the harvest on a basket die-cut. Adhere the die-cuts to your pages or tuck them into pockets on the pages.

Building Off of Journaling Blocks

Using complementary and contrasting colors, cut *journaling blocks* (squares, rectangles, and other geometric shapes) out of paper. You can also buy journaling blocks pre-cut. Write on the blocks of paper and adhere them to your pages. Some scrapbookers even sew on their journaling blocks by hand, and many use their blocks for titles.

Pocketing Secrets Away

Got secrets? You can stash away your really personal journaling in pocket pages. Just put a little slit in the page protector and tuck your journaling card on top of the page — face down or folded. You may want to attach the card to the scrapbook page so that the card doesn't get misplaced.

Handwriting Favorite Recipes

Journal your best recipes in your own handwriting. For example, we'd love to have our grandmother/great-grandmother Minnie Berg's Swedish pancake recipe written in her own hand. *But* we don't have it (probably a good thing too — that sugar, cream, and butter did some major damage!). We do have a picture (1931) of Minnie in her kitchen, and the recipe (which is way too small to read) sits right beside her picture on the page — a page that always brings back great memories of the smells and tastes and fun we had on Saturdays in Minnie's kitchen.

Saying It with Stickers

Many manufacturers make colorful, creative, easy-to-use journaling stickers. Choose the styles and colors that go with your themes and designs. Be sure to write on the sticker *before* you adhere it to your scrapbook page. Then place the sticker on the page, peel it, lightly adhere the sticker to the page, and *burnish* it.

To *burnish* a sticker, place a piece of paper over the sticker and rub the sticker onto the page.

Playing Tag . . .

You're it! So, why not write about you! Write on tags and attach them to your pages — write a little or a lot (tag sizes vary considerably). Write on both sides of the tags (but *not* on both sides of paper, remember!). You can even embellish tags with eyelets, twine, ribbons, and other such stuff. Cut your tags by hand or with a die machine. You can also buy pre-made tags in packages. Some tags are adhesive-backed so that you simply stick them on the page.

Just write, right!

If you want to journal right on your scrapbook page, go for it. Or, write your heart out on whole sheets of paper and put them into page protectors as part of your album. Tell your stories whatever way you want to tell them. And please, use a pen made with ink that will last (refer to Chapter 7).

Chapter 9

Surfing Ten (Okay, Twelve) Tantalizing Scrapbooking Web Sites

In This Chapter

▶ Finding out the "when and where" of scrapbooking conventions

▶ Shopping online for materials, ideas, and techniques

▶ Surfing for scrapping buddies

*I*f you looked for information on scrapbooking before 1997, you didn't have much luck. But, today, if you type **scrapbooking** into a search engine, such as Yahoo or Google, you're directed to approximately 7,000 scrapbooking sites. In response to the overwhelming number of requests for more scrapbooking information, ideas, and products, scrapbook entrepreneurs have created sites to match every scrapper's needs. They've also included scrapbook community builders, such as chat rooms, forums, swapping sites (where you can trade scrapbooking products with others), and scrapbook clubs.

You can shop online, learn scrapbooking techniques, see what's new, ask questions, get answers, and — you name it!

Scrapbooking information flows fast, furiously, and freely over the Internet. Scrapbookers all over the world communicate with one another, sharing ideas, inspiration, and tips. This list of sites is a guide to shopping, consumer magazines that are full of great page ideas, the big scrapbooking conventions, and sites that will link you to many other scrapbooking sites.

Creative Scrapbooking

Posts a calendar of events, tips and ideas, layout galleries, message boards, and even a store directory. A great resource for information regarding the entire scrapbooking industry. (www.creativescrapbooking.com)

Great American Scrapbook Company

Posts information and dates about the Great American Scrapbook Company's (GASC) conventions — the world's largest scrapbook conventions. Held throughout the U.S., GASC offers over 100 educational workshops, cropping parties, *makes and takes* (make a page and take it with you), and more, at every show. A great place to shop, to crop, and to pick up new tips and techniques. (www.greatamerican scrapbook.com)

Luv 2 Scrapbook

This site is one of our favorites. It features over 10,000 products (new products are added daily), a message board, a designer gallery, and much more. A *must-not* miss. (www. luv2scrapbook.com)

My Scrapbook Store Corporation

Everything you'll ever need to create great scrapbook pages. Products from paper to organizational tools that help you stay on the right track. Easy to navigate. (www.myscrapbookstore. com)

Organized Scrapbooks.com

A helpful site when you're organizing your scrapbooking projects. Includes printable forms, articles, links, and even a scrapbook dictionary for those who want to learn scrapbooking terminology. (www.organizedscrapbooks.com)

Scrapbooking About.com

Jam-packed with valuable scrapbooking information that covers a broad scope. Nearly everything is covered here: links to a wide variety of resources, poems and quotes, fonts, book reviews, and techniques such as paper-piecing and chalking. (www.scrapbooking.about.com)

Scrapbooking Top50

Use this site to find sites that are specific to your needs. Hundreds of links listed here, each including a brief description of what you'll find at that Web site. (www.scrapbookingtop50.com)

Scrapjazz LLC

Lots of resources for everyone here, plus an online community, product critiques, contests, magazine and book reviews, articles, design concepts, and much more. (www.scrapjazz.com)

Scraps Ahoy Inc.

Includes a large store, a learning center that disseminates information on techniques, articles, reviews, product and designer spotlights, and links to other scrapbooking Web sites. (www.scrapsahoy.com)

Scrap Town

Offers an online classroom where tips, techniques, contests, and links are right at your fingertips. Easy to navigate. (www.scraptown.com)

Scrap Village.com

Features a fun, informative community, great "General Store" articles, magazine reviews, and message boards where you can interact with other scrappers. (www.scrapvillage.com)

Two Peas in a Bucket Inc.

A variety of resources for scrapbookers of all levels. Features many of the latest scrapbooking products, message boards, forums, and how-to articles on stamping, photography, and other techniques. (www.twopeasinabucket.com)

Getting caught up in the Internet scrapbooking world is easy to do. The information is attractive, fun, and — there's so much of it. Remind yourself to get your workspace organized and to try out some of those great ideas by devoting time to actually scrapbooking.

Be sure to visit your local scrapbook stores in person, too. Store associates are eager to help you by demonstrating tools, materials, and techniques on the spot. You can also attend workshops and classes at the stores and at the major scrapbook conventions, where the vendors' booths are hubs of buzz and activity.

Index

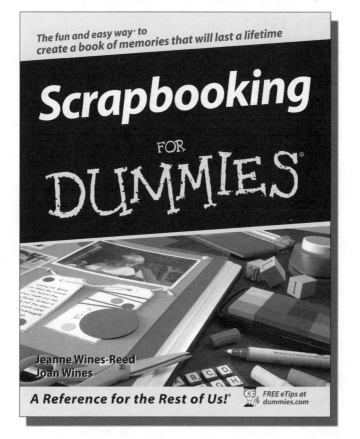

Ultra•PRO® PRODUCTS

8¹/₂ x 11

Consumer Refill Packs

8¹/₂ x 11 Sheet Protectors
#53001

**White Paper with
8¹/₂ x 11 Sheet Protectors**
10 Pages: #57219

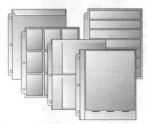

Assorted Photo Refills • 2¹/₂ x 3¹/₂ , 5 x 7,
8 x 10, Negative, Storage Sheet Pages
2 of each Pages: #51510

**Consumer Digital
Refill Pack**

8¹/₂ x 11 Digital Refill
(10) 8¹/₂ x 11 Glossy Ink Jet Photo Paper
(5) 8¹/₂ x 11 Photo Refills
(1) CD Index Print Page
#71047

12 x 12

**Scrapbook Sleeve
Photo Refill**

**Scrapbook Sleeve
Photo Refill**
(10) Scrapbook Sleeves
#54002

**White Paper with
Sheet Protectors**
(10) Papers (5) Sheet Protectors
#57220

**10 Pack Sheet Protector
Photo Refill**
(10) Sheet Protectors
#54001

**Scrapbooking For Dummies
8¹/₂ x 11 Mini Starter Kit** #71091
Also Available in 12 x 12 #71092

**Scrapbooking For Dummies
12 x 12 Box Gift Kit**
#71103

visit our website at www.ultrapro.com